Nebraska Children's Home Society has placed thousands of children in loving adoptive homes in our 120+ year history. This moving story of the adoption circle told from the perspective of an adult who was adopted as an infant is a story of lifelong connections. Tears and laughter, fear and longing, confusion and patience all are part of this mystery which unfolds over a period of many years. I was eager to turn each page to follow the journey of one woman's search for connectedness. The story of adoption is about real human relationships and this story, written with humor, honesty, understanding and insight, captures the essence of meaningful relationships.

Karen Authier, CEO,
Nebraska Children's Home Society

Family Medical History: UNKNOWN/ADOPTED

Family Medical History: UNKNOWN/ADOPTED

How a routine inquiry led to unexpected answers for an adopted woman

Nancy Kacirek Feldman & Rebecca Crofoot

Becknan Publishing

Omaha, Nebraska

ISBN13: 978-1-936840-90-8

Library of Congress Control Number: 2014941528

Author's Note: The people and incidents described in this book are real. In a few cases pseudonyms have been used to preserve anonymity. The original photographs are from the collections of the authors. Permission was obtained by the Nebraska Children's Home Society for the use of images bearing their name.

Printed in the USA

10 9 8 7 6 5 4 3 2 1

Contents

Foreword

Search and reunion is more than what people see in movies or on the daily talk shows. There is a process that adopted persons, birth parents/family, and adoptive parents go through when any member of the adoption circle begins a search. Education is paramount during this process. Thoughts and feelings begin to emerge that those involved in the search may not have even known existed.

Our goal at the Nebraska Children's Home Society is to provide education and support to all members of the adoption circle during and after the search and possible reunion process. We truly do see ourselves as partners in this journey.

I began working in the field of adoption in March 1998 at another licensed child placing agency in Omaha. Prior to this, I worked as a therapist, a licensed mental health practitioner, providing counseling to children and families. Little did I know that I would be embarking on a career that would become and is truly my passion.

I met Becky Crofoot in the spring of 1998, as she was a part of a long-standing group that we still refer to as Search. Search consists of professionals from the other licensed child placing agencies who meet monthly to process ways to locate adopted persons or birth families, to discuss difficult situations (while retaining confidentiality), and to advocate on behalf of all members of the adoption circle. This group over the years has testified in front of the Nebraska Legislature about legislation involving post adoption.

I began working for the Nebraska Children's Home Society in November 2004 and in September 2005 became the Pregnancy, Parenting, and Adoption Program Director. In 2009, I became Becky's supervisor. I learned of Nancy Feldman through my supervision with Becky, and I remember Becky saying that Nancy would be with her until she retired. I remember being impressed with Nancy's ability to process each step of her journey with grace and understanding.

Nancy's experience is a tribute to the partnership that she and Becky formed over the seventeen years they worked together. Nancy eloquently writes about her thoughts and feelings at each step of the process of requesting the Nebraska Children's Home Society to conduct a search for her birth mother. Her journey is significant in that she has the ability to process her thoughts and feelings and that she utilized the education and support from Becky over the years.

My wish and hope for everyone that we are fortunate enough to work with is to see us as partners and continue to use us as a resource, just as Nancy has done.

Nebraska Children's Home Society is a unique agency for many reasons; however, the Nebraska Children's Home Society is the only agency in the country that has not charged fees related to adoption for over a hundred twenty years. The agency has been blessed with adopted persons, birth families, adoptive parents, and others who have given back to the agency with their time, talent, and treasures to support us in our mission of providing safe and loving care to children of all ages.

Kimberly Anderson
Pregnancy, Parenting and Adoption Program Director
Nebraska Children's Home Society

Introduction

This story developed over a period of seventeen years between a caseworker, Rebecca (Becky) Crofoot, and her client, Nancy Feldman. Rebecca was a caseworker for the Nebraska Children's Home Society working in Post Adoption Services when Nancy contacted her in 1994.

Nancy (then Kacirek) had been placed for adoption through that agency in 1949. In 1994, Nancy requested some information from the Nebraska Children's Home Society about her background from the agency, and Rebecca was assigned to her case.

The contacts and correspondence between the two authors from that point on comprise much of the story. Through the years a personal relationship developed, and we felt that Nancy's experience was worthwhile to share with others.

This story takes places between the years of 1994 and 2011 and unfolds through a collection of letters and thoughts through those years. In retrospect, we both added comments from our own perspective. With respect for the privacy of some individuals involved with this story, names, locations, and dates have been changed. The story remains true.

This is a human interest story but also one that provides insight into the emotional rollercoaster of exploring an unknown past. The emotions illustrated throughout the story transcend all age groups and translate to similar experiences. The hope is that this true story will help others whose lives have been touched by adoption to know that their feelings are normal and that the journey is worthwhile no matter what the outcome.

This book was written with the approval of the Nebraska Children's Home Society of Omaha, Nebraska. Without the existence of this incredible facility, this story would literally not have been possible. Our gratitude to NCHS is vast.

Nancy Kacirek Feldman and Rebecca Crofoot

The Journey Begins

It all started in a doctor's office in late March 1994.

Actually, that's not true. It all started back as far as I can remember. I knew that I was loved and that I was adopted. The two meant the same thing to me. I felt that I had a more expansive history than most because a good friend of my mom's named Byrle worked in obstetrics at Omaha's Methodist Hospital. In fact, Byrle was in the delivery room when I was born. But I'm getting ahead of myself, let's return to that L.A. doctor's office in late March 1994.

Until that time I had always thought why worry about my birth parents' medical history? Why have something else to worry about getting? When asked if I wanted to find my family, I used to say, "I don't need to know how many of my family is on death row." I knew that my birth mother had died shortly after I was born, but I had been reassured growing up that my birth had not been the reason for her death.

So I'm sitting practically naked on the exam table, and my current doctor said, obviously frustrated, "You don't know anything about your medical history? Nothing at all?"

I truly never thought that there was going to be a need for a family medical history. But I went through a battery of tests in the 1970s to discover I had mitral valve prolapse. That was not supposed to be an inherited trait, but my son was diagnosed with it in the 1980s. Now I was having another health issue, and I was beginning to believe that I should find out whatever I could.

"No, nothing more than what I told you," I said. "My parents were both in their late twenties, my birth mother died and my father was in the military and had no one to help with me, so he gave me up for adoption. My mother was a nurse from somewhere in the Midwest. Minnesota, I think. He was from the South. Arkansas, maybe Alabama. It was an 'A' state, but southern. Oh, and I had to be readmitted to the hospital at two weeks of age because I wouldn't eat. Don't they call that failure to thrive now?"

My doctor looked at me oddly, obviously thinking that I, at age forty-five and clearly not malnourished, was legions away from a failure-to-thrive case. He sighed, "It would be really helpful if we had something, anything. It might help to explain the mitral valve prolapse or the interstitial cystitis. Can you get anything? Were you a private adoption or orphanage?"

"Nebraska Children's Home in Omaha was where I came from. I think they are still around. They would have records if anyone did," I said.

"Would you be willing to contact them?"

And, simple as that, my search started.

-0-

It felt weird, but I went ahead. I was excited, but I also thought, *You could be asking for a whole lot of trouble.* I decided not to tell my folks for two reasons. I didn't want them to be worried about my physical maladies, thinking that it must be really bad if I have to dig up my family medical history. And I didn't want them to think that in any way that I was looking for my "real" family. My mom's health was fragile. She had been experiencing mini-strokes and was having periods of paranoia. I didn't want to add to her woes.

The first letter was typed out on April 8, 1994, and sent to the Nebraska Children's Home on Fontenelle Boulevard in Omaha. While I lived in Omaha, I had been by the place many times, but in only once. My Girl Scout troop made a St. Valentine's visit to kids that were living there. At least I think they were living there. We brought valentines and cookies. I remember getting all shy suddenly, thinking I could have been one of those kids getting the valentines. I was thinking a lot of different thoughts while I typed:

> To Whom It Will Concern:
>
> I am one of your former adoption "graduates"! I have been diagnosed with a medical condition and various treatments have been proposed to me. My 21 year old son has also been found to have the same condition. Never having had a family medical background has been something that I just didn't concern myself with, but more recently I have felt that it is important that I have this information both for myself and my son. Our physician has urged me to seek out my family medical history in order to help clarify this current medical problem and be mindful of others that might influence our future health status. Since my adoption was handled through your organization, I am hopeful that you have records that contain my birth family medical history.
>
> My birth certificate stated that I was born Nancy Elaine Kacirek on January 26, 1949, (no time listed), at the Methodist Hospital in Omaha, Nebraska, to George and Lucille Kacirek. From the Decree of Adoption issued by the County Court of Douglas County, Nebraska, I understand that I was born Baby Girl Carroll.

If there is any additional paperwork that I need to complete in order to process my request, please contact me at the address listed below.

Thank you.

Sincerely,

Nancy Kacirek Feldman

I had sudden feelings of panic and wanted to receive the answer immediately to a letter that I had not even mailed. My husband, Michael, took it from there and said, "Give it to me and I will fax it from work."

We went back and forth about this for a couple of days. I couldn't believe that I was now having feelings that I didn't want to let go of the letter then. He took it to work on April 11, and I called twice to see if he had faxed it yet.

The fax transmittal sheet was dated 4/11 and the time 12:20 PST. Michael was then working for a company in Long Beach. Michael had called Nebraska Children's Home and gotten the fax number. He wrote on the cover sheet: "As per our discussion attached letter gives information for search. Please call me if you have any questions. Thanks for your help. Michael Feldman."

Nothing was heard on the eleventh, but I tried to console myself that there was a two-hour time difference. The next day Michael called me at the office and asked if I had any plans for lunch.

"Did you get a response?" was the only thing I could say.

He would just answer, "I'll be over to get you in about thirty minutes."

At that time, Michael and I had been married seventeen years and he knew me well. We met in 1974, when I moved back from rural Michigan to Los Angeles to live with my parents. My first marriage had ended after three and a half years. I was sharing a great old house with two other women and my toddler, Forrest. I liked my job in medical records in the small community hospital, the people I worked with and small town life in general. But I was recognizing that my parents were not getting any benefit from their only child and only grandchild living so far away.

So I made the call and asked to be able to come home. My parents were both so welcoming. Forrest and I lived with them for two years. At times it was not easy, as in the quote, "If mom says no, ask Grandma!" I was living that quote. But Forrest thrived in that adoring environment.

Michael had been married nine years and had a five-year-old daughter. When we married, we knew that we would experience some ups and downs, and we did. Most days were a combination of the two, but all in all, leaving Michigan and returning to LA gave me the opportunity to continue the charmed life I've had.

Going to work at Harbor–UCLA Medical Center in 1976 had been a great decision. I was paid a decent wage and unbelievable benefits. I had started working in pediatrics in 1980 and had found my niche. I loved the pediatrician mind set. Cue Joe Walsh to sing, "Life's been good to me so far."

By the time of my adoption search in 1994, I was working in the Perinatal Research Projects at Harbor–UCLA. Michael picked me up at work and drove straight to one of our favorite Mexican food places, Acapulco on Carson Street. He did not give me the fax until we were seated and ordered our food. It was all going so slowly. I was in agony. Then he handed it to me and I hurriedly read the faxed letter:

> April 12, 1994
>
> Dear Nancy:
>
> We hope that things are going well for you and that you will be back on your feet soon. Your record does not have a great deal of medical information in it but what it does contain may be significant.

> Your birth mother was said to have been in "good health" as were her siblings. Her mother had died when your birth mother was 4 years old. She died from hemorrhaging after the "removal of a fibroid tumor." It was stressed that this was not cancerous. Her father died of cancer at the age of 48. The record does not indicate anything more specific.
>
> Your birth mother knew of no hereditary diseases in your birth father's family. This is essentially all we have by way of history. If we can do anything more, please let us know.

The fax was signed by someone who was designated as a staff person.

I sat there in shock. "She didn't die," I kept saying to which Michael continued to reply, "It would appear so."

"They weren't married."

"No, it sounds like they weren't. Do you think that maybe you should ask your folks about this?" Michael asked.

"No, no, I couldn't. They might think I was betraying them, throwing them out in favor of my 'real' parents. No, no, I can't do that. I don't want them hurt by this."

"Do you think they lied to you?" he asked.

"I don't care. She didn't die! Maybe she's still alive!"

I searched old records that I had to try to make some sense of this startling revelation. The following is the long-awaited letter, stating that my adoption was now official. Probation for adoptive parents, called foster parents then, was one year.

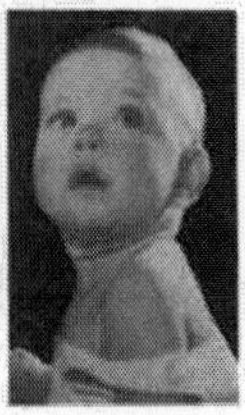

CHARTERED SEPTEMBER 1893

Building futures and providing homes and opportunities for Nebraska's orphaned children—statewide

Nebraska Children's Home Society

3549 FONTENELLE BOULEVARD · PHONE PLEASANT 0787 OMAHA 4, NEBRASKA

April 6th, 1950.

Mr. and Mrs. George W. Kacirek,
1204 South 54th Street,
Omaha, Nebraska.

Dear Mr. and Mrs. Kacirek:

Here are the papers you are waiting for, the papers necessary to complete the adoption of that little girl we placed in your home. Take these papers to your attorney for completion and filing. He will then file them in the Douglas County Court and Judge Troyer will set a hearing not earlier than four weeks nor later than eight from that date. The three of you must appear in Court for the hearing at which time the decree will be entered. Please see that we receive a certified copy of the decree promptly.

When the adoption is completed our supervision will actually cease and this little girl will be entirely yours. Although our supervision will cease, our interest in the welfare of the Kacirek family will continue throughout the years and we hope that you will always feel yourselves to be important members of this great big family known as the Nebraska Children's Home Society which exists solely to make others happy.

In placing this little girl with you we expressed our confidence that you would provide the kind of home, the right kind of guidance and the opportunities which will help her to grow into the kind of woman which all the world admires. We hope that as the years roll on that confidence will be vindicated and in turn, we hope this little girl will measure up to your hopes and respond in full measure to your love, your guidance and the opportunities you have to offer.

Being a parent is a wonderful opportunity and a great privilege; one that brings with it heavy responsibilities as well. There will be days in the years ahead when all your patience, all your skill and all your understanding may be needed but we feel that you will rise to meet every situation. May the years ahead carry a full measure of happiness, good health and success to you all.

Cordially yours,
NEBRASKA CHILDREN'S HOME SOCIETY.

Randall C. Biart
Executive Director.

P. S. Be sure to tell this little lassie that she has been adopted as soon as she is old enough to understand.
RCB:GS

NCHS Executive Director's letter to my parents, April 6, 1950

Excited about the news that my birth mother had not died, I suddenly desired to have my original and amended birth certificates.

I knew nothing of the 1994 laws and was still in a daze from my recent discovery, but thought why not? I sent a check for $16, which was the price for two certificates.

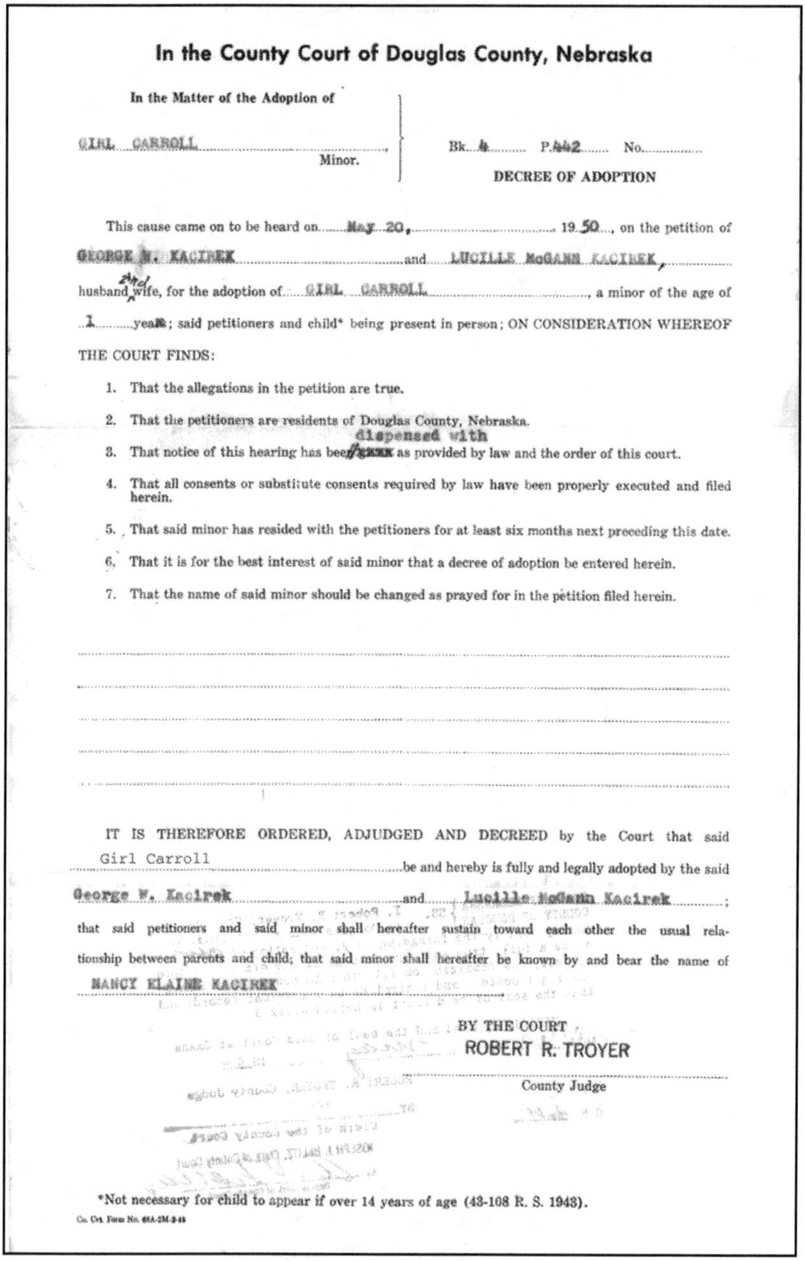

In the County Court of Douglas County, Nebraska

In the Matter of the Adoption of

GIRL CARROLL, Minor.

Bk. 4 P. 442 No.

DECREE OF ADOPTION

This cause came on to be heard on May 20, 1950, on the petition of GEORGE W. KACIREK and LUCILLE McCANN KACIREK, husband and wife, for the adoption of GIRL CARROLL, a minor of the age of 1 year; said petitioners and child* being present in person; ON CONSIDERATION WHEREOF THE COURT FINDS:

1. That the allegations in the petition are true.
2. That the petitioners are residents of Douglas County, Nebraska.
3. That notice of this hearing has been dispensed with as provided by law and the order of this court.
4. That all consents or substitute consents required by law have been properly executed and filed herein.
5. That said minor has resided with the petitioners for at least six months next preceding this date.
6. That it is for the best interest of said minor that a decree of adoption be entered herein.
7. That the name of said minor should be changed as prayed for in the petition filed herein.

IT IS THEREFORE ORDERED, ADJUDGED AND DECREED by the Court that said Girl Carroll be and hereby is fully and legally adopted by the said George W. Kacirek and Lucille McCann Kacirek; that said petitioners and said minor shall hereafter sustain toward each other the usual relationship between parents and child; that said minor shall hereafter be known by and bear the name of NANCY ELAINE KACIREK

BY THE COURT

ROBERT R. TROYER

County Judge

*Not necessary for child to appear if over 14 years of age (43-108 R. S. 1943).

Co. Crt. Form No. 66A-2M-3-48

My official Decree of Adoption, May 20, 1950.

I received a letter from the State of Nebraska Department of Health, which was dated April 22. The form letter came back with a check for $8, as well as a certified copy of my birth certificate. I was told that the first birth certificate had been closed at the time my adoptive birth certificate was filed. If I were to obtain a written release from my birth parent or have proof that they had passed, I would be able to see this closed birth certificate. All of this made me realize I was not going to get any more information without help.

My mom had started having personality changes in the early 1980s. In appearance, she was still my mom, but her actions and words were from an angry, paranoid, bitter individual. I tried several ways to break this barrier with my mom with no success.

It wasn't until 1989, when Mom had a major stroke, that we learned she had been having mini-strokes all those years. But long before that, I realized I couldn't change my mom's behavior, but I could change the way I reacted to her through counseling.

With all of this sudden news flash, I turned to Georgia Cox, my therapist, for help. She had some recommendations for adoption searches. It was quite a list of attorneys, search and support personnel, and support groups. One of the individuals listed had found her father. Suddenly I had a lot to talk to Georgia about. It was thrilling and scary. Where was this going to lead? I realized that going back to the Nebraska Children's Home was the best solution.

Looking back on the sequence of events, there are places where an explanation or some clarification could be helpful for the reader. These comments will appear periodically as "Becky's Note."

Becky's Note: *Although original birth certificates are sealed in Nebraska, the state law provides several ways to access the records. The placing agency is required to aid in that process, which may mean a* *search for birth relatives. Birth parents can give their consent (or non-consent) to the opening of the original birth certificate and/or for contact with the adopted person. Because the law was passed many years after Nancy's birth in 1949, it could be assumed that her birth parents would not be aware of the law and how it might affect them. Since there was nothing on file at the State of Nebraska, the next step for Nancy was to turn to the agency where I was a caseworker.*

And so on April 28, 1994, I composed the following letter:

Hello again:

I want to take this opportunity to thank you for helping me collect my family medical history. You were very helpful to both my husband, Michael, and me, and I want you to know we do appreciate it.

I have a condition called interstitial cystitis. Its cause is unknown and it can be life altering. I am fortunately in a remission phase now. In addition, both my son Forrest, now aged 21 years, and I have a heart condition labeled mitral valve prolapse. It is not supposed to be congenital, and so our physician encouraged me to investigate my family medical history and felt any link to the past might prove very helpful in further understanding both of these ailments. Both Forrest and I have to be mindful of some physical restrictions and medication precautions now, but it is hoped that the MVP's general impact on our lives will be slight. I believed that there might be a connection with my past with this, and hence I made the inquiry.

You see I believed that my birth mother had died shortly after my birth and that my birth father had been the one to give me up for adoption. However, upon receipt of your communication I learned that my birth mother had been alive at the time of my adoption and was most likely the individual who put me up for adoption. It was a lot to learn that what I had thought all my life was possibly someone else's story. My mom is the one who provided me with the information and it is very likely that she was given misinformation in error. She believed that I was born at the hospital where she had worked (the Methodist) and her friends, who still worked there, had called her excitedly about a baby that was going to the Nebraska Children's Home and must surely be her baby. Her good friend was the assisting nurse in the delivery room, and she pleaded with her, "Lucille, I am certain that this is going to be your baby."

She resisted the temptation to come up to the hospital to see this baby, but accepted all the information provided by her friends: The couple was married. The birth mother was a nurse, the birth father in the military. The birth mother died after childbirth. Years later I would see a television drama where a baby's birth had allegedly caused the mother's death. The father held this against the child. I went to my mom concerned that this had also been my case, but she reassured me that my case was different.

I was told that my birth mother's body was sent home to Minnesota. The birth father was from the south. They were in their late 20's, both had dark hair, they were both of medium stature, and the ethnicity was English/Scot's Irish. My questions were answered whenever I raised them, but my parents never sat down and said, "This is your story." This was a lot of information to be gleaned in the late 1940's for an adoption. But I did wonder if just perhaps I was some other baby born about the same time, but was carrying around someone else's story. This goes along with the adopted child's fantasy of being royalty. All adopted children feel a kinship to Moses, given up as a child in order to save him.

I learned also that I had to be readmitted to the hospital at two weeks of age as I was refusing to eat. Of course, I was admitted to the Methodist, and somehow Byrle was aware that I was there. It's probably because I had to be in the nursery as I was so young. In March, my parents were notified, "Congratulations, you are parents!" All family and friends came to the house and Byrle and Dottie who were both at the Methodist, declared, "Just as we thought in January, here's your baby!"

At first when your letter arrived I was a little shocked. It took a few days for me to digest the information that what I thought was my background was not, but as the days passed I became comfortable with having a mystery background. It just took some time to adjust. I attribute this acceptance to the fact that I was raised in love by two people whom I truly deem as my parents.

From my earliest remembrances I knew that I was loved and adopted. Your agency did a marvelous job in matching me with the most wonderful of parents. I honor and cherish them. In addition, I honor those who gave me life and made the decision to put me up for adoption. I believe people give children up for important reasons and that their decisions and feelings should be respected. I am not an advocate of tracking down birth parents. Adoption is a highly charged emotional situation on both sets of parents and deserves special handling. I have no intention of trying to drag my birth parents into my life.

Now that I am the mystery lady, I do have just a few questions. What information, other than medical history, am I entitled to request without jeopardizing the confidentiality of my birth parents? I wonder if I can be provided ethnicity background, ages of birth parents and the time of my birth (I couldn't understand why the time was left off of the birth certificate). Will you let me know if I am entitled to such information? As before, I appreciate your assistance. If you wish, you can reply to me at my work fax number.

I am pleased to know that I will now be on the mailing list of NCHS. It was like discovering I belonged to a club that I never knew I was a member of. Not many agencies have reached such a grand old age as NCHS. I am certainly grateful for your existence. You provided me with a wonderful life.

Thank you.

Sincerely,

Nancy Kacirek Feldman

Becky's Note: *In today's world we know how vital having a comprehensive medical history is to our well-being. However, that was not always true in the past. There was very little documentation of health history at the time Nancy was born. So many conditions that we know to be important today were simply not diagnosed at that time. Also, medical attention was not readily available to many people and treatment was not sought. Thus, many records hold little or no medical history and often the information that was* *available at that time is not relevant today because of the expansion of medical knowledge.*

The Nebraska Children's Home Society provides continual services for adopted persons and birth parents as well as adoptive families for no cost. The Service Philosophy is provided to the client for the purpose of explaining the agency's commitment to being available to the client.

SERVICE PHILOSOPHY FOR POST ADOPTION SERVICES

The purpose of the Post Adoption Services at the Nebraska Children's Home Society is to provide continuing support and education in order to encourage open, honest and timely relationships between all of the members of the adoption circle. We are committed to the belief that the experience of adoption has life-long implications for all involved and may affect them in many different ways. This service recognizes the importance of the feelings of all members of the adoption circle but the ultimate goal is to enhance the life of the adopted person.

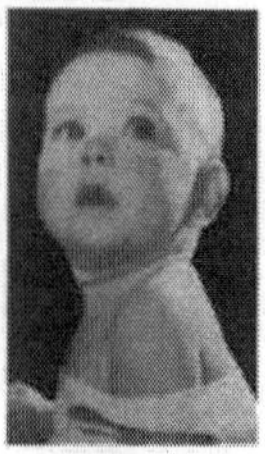

CHARTERED 1893

Nebraska Children's Home Society

3549 Fontenelle Boulevard — Omana, Nebraska 68104

(402) 451-0787 — FAX (402) 451-0360

A Private Non-sectarian Agency Providing Adoption Services • Temporary Foster Care • Services to Single Pregnant Women • Emergency Shelter Care

May 18, 1994

Dear Nancy:

I enjoyed your letter and also the fact that you have been provided with background history by your parents. You will find this all very interesting as it does fit the enclosed history. There are some major differences though, especially the death of your birth mother. Our records certainly indicate that she was fine and had plans to apply for a job, etc.

We have often found that adopted people (or their parents) were told that a birth parent died out of some attempt at kindness. Generally, our agency wasn't guilty of that but it's quite possible. It could have been the hospital also. Anyway, it's very interesting!

If you are interested in pursuing this further please let me know. I'm enclosing a brochure about searching which may answer some questions for you.

Sincerely,
Nebraska Children's Home Society
Rebecca Crofoot
Caseworker

HISTORY: NANCY KACIREK FELDMAN

You were born on January 26, 1949, at 11:33 a.m. at the Methodist Hospital in Omaha, Nebraska. You weighed 7 lbs. 4 ½ oz. Your birth was normal.

Your birth mother was born and reared in the Midwest. When she was 4 years of age, her mother died leaving six children, four girls and twin boys. Her father tried to take care of the family with housekeeping services. This lasted for three years when he did remarry. Your birth mother's stepmother was a wonderful woman and did have a very prestigious job. Our records do indicate that your birth mother had commented that there could never have been a better mother in the world to the children than her stepmother, who was still living at the time and whom she felt as much love for as though she were her biological mother.

The stepmother was largely responsible for seeing that the girls had nursing training. Three were graduate nurses and one was a graduate of a business college. Your birth mother's father had died when your birth mother was 11 years old.

After your birth mother came out of nurses training, she went immediately into the United States Army as a nurse. She met your birth father, who was a Lieutenant in the Army. They did go together for

Nebraska Children's Home Society Post Legal Adoption Services brochure.

nearly a year, but he had moved before the pregnancy was discovered. Your birth mother made no attempt whatsoever to get in touch with him about the pregnancy stating she did not want to hamper his career.

At the time of your birth, your birth mother was 28 years old. She was 5'1" tall and weighed 105 lbs. She had grayish dark blue eyes, black naturally curly hair and a fair complexion. She did mention that the average height of the women in her family were about 5'5" tall. She was the smallest. None of them were heavyset.

Your birth mother went through high school and then on to her nurses training. She liked English and history best in high school, and she described herself as being an average student.

According to our records, your birth mother was not especially musically inclined although she did enjoy semi-classical and classical music. Her hobby was collecting poetry. She also was very interested in nursing, feeling that she chose the right field of work. She enjoyed tennis and swimming. Her health was excellent. She belonged to the Episcopal Church.

One of your birth mother's sisters was living in a nearby community. She was married to a young doctor. This brother-in-law and sister had been very kind to her and helped her make plans to come to Omaha. She planned to return to their home until she regained her strength.

Your birth mother's three sisters were fair to medium in complexion. Three of the girls had black hair and one auburn hair. All had naturally curly hair. The brothers had medium complexion and dark brown curly hair. Both brothers were serving in the Army.

Your birth mother's mother was 5'5" and weighed between 115 and 120 lbs. She had hazel eyes, black hair and a fair complexion. She was of Scottish and Irish descent. She graduated from high school and did have further education. Previous to her marriage she was a principal of a high school.

Your birth mother's mother was said to be of a very quiet temperament, but extremely well thought of in the community. The cause of her death was a hemorrhage following the removal of a fibroid tumor. There were no hereditary diseases in her background.

Your birth mother's father was 5'11" and weighed 165–170 lbs. He had blue eyes and black hair. He also was of Scottish and Irish descent. He was a high school graduate and had continued his education. Prior to marriage, he was a high school superintendent.

Your birth mother felt that her father was quite a remarkable man. His parents were large ranchers and were considered very prominent people. After your birth mother's father left teaching, he did have some fairly high political jobs. He died at the age of 48. The cause of his death was cancer. Your birth mother remembered him as always having an optimistic spirit about everything. He was very much loved and respected by the members of the community.

Your birth father was 27 years old. He was 5'9" or 5'10" tall and weighed about 130 lbs. He had dark brown naturally curly hair and blue eyes. He had a medium complexion. He was of English descent. He was a high school graduate and did have the equivalent of two years of college. He was a 1st Lieutenant in the Army. He was probably above average in intelligence, did not have any special talents, but had an exceptional pleasing personality.

Nebraska Children's Home located at 3549 Fontenelle Blvd.

Your birth mother really knew very little about your birth father's family. However, he did speak of his father being a farmer, also that he had one brother who was killed in action. This brother had received various medals for bravery. There was also one younger brother in the Merchant Marines.

Because of her circumstances and that there were no plans of marriage, your birth mother felt it would be in your best interest to make adoptive plans for you.

First Shock, Then Questions

WOW! I can't believe all of this has happened. And I can't believe how much information was in my file! I can't believe I know so much now.

WOW again!

Becky's Note: *Nancy's reaction to the background information is typical and quite appropriate. She had happily ignored that piece of her whole being for most of her life. Seeing a previously unknown history in writing can be a startling experience. After incorporating the initial shock, more questions began to emerge.*

June 14, 1994

Ms. Rebecca Crofoot
Nebraska Children's Home Society
Dear Rebecca:

I must immediately thank you for your warm letter and my background information. How many times can I tell you how delighted and fascinated I was with such detailed and complete information? I never dreamed of getting such a story. I have happily carried your letter and the background information with me ever since I received and have read and re-read it again. It certainly reads like a romance novel! I don't believe I ever appreciated my curly hair as much as I do now after learning that everyone in my background had curly hair! And it is uncanny how well my background was matched to that of my parents. All over again, I am grateful to NCHS for a perfect match. And as I look at your letterhead I see that my Omaha childhood pediatrician is on the Board of Trustees! I feel very connected to NCHS.

I am still somewhat overcome by the discovery that my birth mother did not die after my birth. I bear no ill will to whoever decided to give me that information and have accepted it, as you said, as having been done out of kindness. And yet it was a startling finding to make after 45 years. Adopted children are a fascination to many and I have found most people want to encourage "us" to find our "real" parents. I personally chose not to do that since I believed that my birth father had given me up for adoption, and I thought that just possibly he had blamed me for my birth mother's death. It seemed to me that it would be unfair to break into my birth father's life with a part of his past that he might well want to forget ever happened just to satisfy some curiosity that I felt about my background.

Knowing now that my birth mother had elected not to tell him of my existence makes me ever more resolved not to attempt a contact with my birth father. I will honor her wishes. However, after studying my background, I did experience an outpouring of warm feeling and awe towards my birth mother. I suddenly wanted to be able to find out just where in the Midwest she had lived, to go there and observe her home, places her family had worked, look at pictures of her family etc. And I wanted to send a note to her in essence thanking her for not only providing me with life, but for gifting two strangers with a gift that they so desperately wanted: a child. I wanted her to know that I had been a happy child and was a contented adult. And yet I have held back because I still do not know whether I have the right to intrude into her life, even if by only a note.

My existence may very well have been a secret between sisters. Also, the possibility exists that she may be no longer living. In that case, if a contact were attempted, I would worry about upsetting the children she might have had, who might not have been told of my existence. But I still found myself wanting to make contact.

On the other hand, I ask myself, "Is it necessary to reassure her after all these years that I am fine?" In reading of her love for her stepmother, I do believe that she knew that I would be loved and cherished because she knew that a blood bond is not required to love a child as one's own. I am obviously at a crossroads of thought with this as I want to still protect my birth mother's privacy, but the fantasy of contacting her is a pleasurable one.

I read with interest the brochure on Post Legal Adoption Services. I don't think I am totally clear about the Vital Statistics Bureau's policy on obtaining one's birth certificate for beginning a search. I think it states that at the time my birth was registered, my birth mother could have elected to close the file so as to prevent any searching. But it also states that if both parents are listed on the birth certificate, then both must be contacted before the original certificate can be released.

I am only guessing, but it seems as if both my birth parents are listed on this document as my adoption papers bear the last name of CARROLL, which is traditionally an English name. Since my birth father's background was English, and my birth mother's background was Scottish and Irish, it would seem that is my birth father's name. This would stop any attempt on my part to conduct a search as it would mean my birth father would have to be contacted and that would go against my birth mother's wishes.

In trying to think this out, I believe the safest route (meaning to protect both birth parents) to attempt any search would be to go through my birth mother's sister, who at the time of my birth lived in a nearby community to Omaha. If she is no longer living or no longer in the area, that route would be moot as well. What a tremendous amount to dwell on!

I have thrown a lot at you, I know, but I ask for your indulgence. I am just so much in awe of all of the information that I have received, and I am just uncertain how much farther I should go. In your experience with searches, did most birth parents welcome contact? In even asking you this I know it must be hard to pin this down with statistics because I am certain each case is as individual as the person involved. Was there any notation in my file about my birth mother's feelings about possible future contact from me?

I have the name and telephone of an organization called Families by Adoption here in California and I may call and ask what their experiences have been in searching. Still, it would be relying on statistics of other people's situations. I am obviously wrestling with this and I thank you for bearing with me. I am overwhelmed with my intoxicating background and just felt so moved to extend some warmth out to my birth mother. Much of what I learned from my tale was particularly fascinating because it held a key to some previously unexplained traits and passions of my own. My love of poetry and classical music, I thought, came out of nowhere. It was fascinating to learn these details and understand myself even more.

You work for a non-profit organization and I know exactly what that means. Questions answered, backgrounds prepared, and searches conducted all involve time and that means dollars spent. I imagine your caseload is high and I don't want to further burden you, but I would appreciate your insight into my situation. I have enclosed a donation in the check amount of $100.00. I realize that this is not a great deal, but please know that it is heart felt as my husband, like so many in this nation, is unemployed at this time.

Adoption may be scary to many right now. Last summer's Baby Jessica fiasco pulled at the heartstrings of many of us. I felt awful for the adoptive parents and knew full well how it would have devastated my parents if that had happened to them. I wished that the deciding judge had first consulted a group of adopted children before entering a decision. I want you to feel free to use my statements about how I feel to any and all prospective adoptive parents. Tell them how I honor my birth mother for providing me with the gift of life and then expanded that gift to two strangers. And that I am proud to have been adopted and that I have no questions about whom my real parents are.

After reading my background, my husband smiled at me and said, "I don't think you are done with this,

Nancy." He may be right. I plan to think this through slowly and carefully. It is not my intent to upset anyone's life. If you have anything to add or suggestions to make, I would welcome them. The only thing I am certain about at this time with respect to my search/ or not to search is that if anyone from my birth family wished to contact me through your organization, I would be pleased to hear from him or her.

Rebecca, thank you with all my heart.

Sincerely,

Nancy Kacirek Feldman

Becky's Note: *Nancy was especially cautious about processing the new information before moving on. Each step can be overwhelming and rushing can be disastrous. She wisely chose to move slowly. She also felt the urge to talk to other adopted people as a way to clarify her thoughts. Some people seek support groups, which are available in many areas. In Nancy's case, she discovered individuals all around her with similar experiences. Also, Nancy's husband understood a great deal and he was able to be of valuable support. Often those around the searcher can see the situation more clearly.*

Many adopted people approach the agency by first asking for health history sometimes not realizing that every piece of information they receive opens a new door full of additional questions. Nancy's sudden rush of feelings and anxiety as she began are a glimpse of a realization of things to come. Her inquiry truly began a "journey"—a longer and more complicated walk than she ever imagined.

At this point, Nancy needed to know that her feelings were normal. She also needed to know that the agency was there to help. She was asked to fill out some forms to begin the process to receive specific services.

Aunt Mae Kacirek, my godmother, and me on baptism day at Kountze Memorial Lutheran Church, Omaha, 1949.

A smiling family and baby Nancy on baptism day. From left in front: Cousin Ken Kacirek, Aunt Joyce Kacirek. Back row: Grandpa Joseph Kacirek, Grandma Antoinette Kacirek, Baby Nancy in Aunt Mae Kacirek's arms, Uncle John Kacirek.

The whole family on baptism day. From left in front: Aunt Joyce Kacirek, Cousin Betty Stevens, Cousin Ken Kacirek. Back row: Grandpa Joseph and Grandma Antoinette Kacirek, George Kacirek (my dad), Lucille Kacirek (my mom), Uncle John and Aunt Mae Kacirek (my godparents), and baby Nancy.

Thanksgiving, November 1956 on Whitmore in Minne Lusa. From left, front row: Cousin Ken Kacirek, Nancy Kacirek, my mom, Lucille Kacirek. Back row: Grandpa Joseph and Grandma Antoinette Kacirek, Aunt Mae and Uncle John Kacirek, Grandma Anna and Grandpa Arthur McGann.

A new cousin, and the fourth generation is here! From the left on couch: Aunt Ethel Stevens, Mom and Dad, Lucille and George Kacirek. Front row: Cousin Betty Stevens Dennis, Nancy Kacirek, Cousin Jan Stevens. Second row: Grandma Anna McGann holding her new great grandson, Mark Dennis. Grandpa Arthur McGann. Standing: Cousin Gene Stevens.

Christmas 1957 at Aunt Ethel's in Benson (Omaha). From the left, back row: Cousin Jan Stevens, Aunt Grace Daughtrey, Mom Lucille Kacirek, Aunt Ethel Stevens, Grandpa Arthur McGann. Front row sitting: Nancy Kacirek with her Grandma Anna McGann.

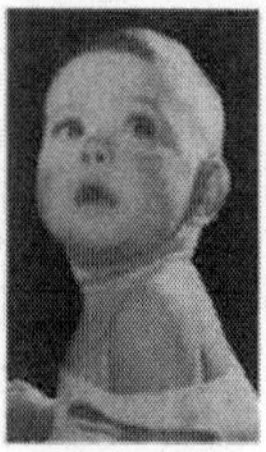

CHARTERED 1893

Nebraska Children's Home Society

3549 Fontenelle Boulevard — Omana, Nebraska 68104
(402) 451-0787 — FAX (402) 451-0360

A Private Non-sectarian Agency Providing Adoption Services • Temporary Foster Care • Services to Single Pregnant Women • Emergency Shelter Care

June 20, 1994

Dear Nancy:

I read with great interest your long letter about your feelings on adoption and learning more of your history. I wished that you were closer to Omaha as we could have a pretty long chat on the subject!

My first thought was to suggest some reading to you, but then I felt that the existing literature is not that appropriate for you. You seem to know your feelings pretty well and your dilemma is not to identify your feelings but to determine what to do with them. I do think books on searching, etc., may be of some interest to you but not all that necessary at this point.

Another thought is to find a local search group and go to one of their meetings. You may find some "kindred spirits" there.

If you wish to just go ahead, fill out the enclosed form and send it to the Bureau of Vital Statistics with the fee. Then, send me a copy of their answer. The law is a recent one and it's unlikely that your birth mother even knows that she has the right to consent or non-consent.

My only other suggestion is to trust your own feelings. Talk about it with people you know and think about it and I think your direction will come!

> Thank you so much for the check. We so appreciate your support of the work that we do. People like you make it possible for us to continue. Thank you!
>
> Sincerely,
> Nebraska Children's Home Society
> Rebecca Crofoot
> Caseworker

Becky's Note: *The Nebraska Children's Home Society did not charge a fee for the information shared with Nancy nor are there fees for any of the work in Post Adoption Services. The agency has a long tradition of being supported solely by contributions, which is very unusual in today's world. Obviously, there is the thought that providing good service to the clients would result in support for the agency's work. Nancy correctly understood the situation and offered a contribution. The future of the agency obviously depends on such contributions.*

Becky sent what was called the REQUEST FOR ACCESS TO BIRTH INFORMATION, and it was a form to be filled out, which I did, and I returned it the Bureau of Vital Statistics in Lincoln, Nebraska. There was nothing special about it. Having worked as a medical secretary for so many years, I had seen, and filled out, my share of forms. But it was a start of an exciting journey. I had no idea where it would lead.

The letter sent in response to mine bore the seal of the State of Nebraska and was dated June 21, 1994, and, of course, it was addressed to me, regarding me. It said, "The completed Request for Access to Birth Information form has been received and will be filed permanently."

I was informed that their office was authorized to release the name of the court granting the adoption and the name of the child placement agency involved, if any, when consent forms of the biological relatives have not been filed or consent forms of the adoptive parents have not been filed. The adoption was granted by the County Court of Douglas County in Omaha, Nebraska.

The letter went on to state, “The name of the child placement agency is not given in our files.” Now that threw me. Why wouldn’t they have that in the files? Hadn’t I told them that?

It also stated that if I wished to do an adoption search, I could contact the Department of Social Services Adoption Coordinator. Another enclosure was a letter of instructions if I wanted to do an adoption search with the Department of Social Services.

I was instructed to present a copy of this letter to the County Court and/or child placement agency as indicated for their further instructions. I thought I understood this. That meant it was to go to the Nebraska Children’s Home. I could do that.

In case of my biological parent’s death, proof (I’m thinking death certificate) would be accepted in lieu of the consent forms. They did offer to help if I thought they were dead. And I was thinking, *But I just found out she was alive!*

The one thing I did understand was that it was signed by a correspondence supervisor and had some enclosures. I was pleased to see that it was printed with soy ink on recycled paper.

I found myself thinking, *What did it say? Would it be too much to ask Rebecca to translate?*

The enclosure also had an official seal of the State of Nebraska and the governor’s name. I remember thinking, *What happened to that governor who dated the* Terms of Endearment *star, Deborah Winger?* [The *Jeopardy!* answer is Governor Bob Kerrey.] That thought didn’t have anything to do with the letter or my search (for what I wasn’t certain yet), but I guess the mind works that way.

It read:

"Instructions to Searchers:

In order to facilitate services to persons wanting to do an adoption search, the Nebraska Department of Social Services requires that you send a written request to: Adoption Search, Department of Social Services." That made sense. I could do that.

I was told that I would need the following:

"A copy of the Nebraska Vital Statistics Response to your inquiry for birth information, if you are at least 25 years of age." Not sure what this is.

"Your adoptive name, present name, address, phone number and birth date." This I could do.

"The names of your adoptive parents." Got it.

"The date of adoption." Didn't have this. Just knew it was March 1949 that they got me. I had seen a court paper with a letter in 1970, but I could not remember the date. On the court paper I was referred to as Baby Carroll. I remember that blew my mind. I said to my mom, "But you never told me that you knew my last name?"

To which she replied, "Nancy, darling girl, all I remember about that letter is that it meant no more unscheduled visits from the agency, no more worries that someone would take you away from me. That letter meant that we had passed our year's probation period and that you were ours free and clear from now on. Your last name was the last thing I was thinking about."

Of course, she could remember what she and I wore to court the day it was finalized. Of course, she could! Because that was about us then—the us that was going on to the future of being the three Kacireks.

The letter went on:

"A statement from your adoptive parents approving your search if you are under 25 years of age." This is not a worry.

"A statement from you (and your adoptive parents if you are under age 25) authorizing the Department of Social Services to release your name, address and phone number to any relative who may wish to know your whereabouts for immediate or future use." Ditto.

"Anything you may know about your birth situation (e.g., Names, addresses, hospitals, attorneys, friends, etc.)." If I had not had the Nebraska Children's Home, I would have needed all of this.

"Request an update in writing 3 months after your first letter." Will I remember this?

And I was told to please call if I had any questions.

This form was also printed on recycled paper, but what happened to the soy ink?

June 27, 1994

Ms. Rebecca Crofoot

Nebraska Children's Home Society

Dear Rebecca:

Thank you for your timely response and warm involvement. I have not only gained a wealth of information about myself in the past few months, but have made, I feel, a new friend. You have been most kind and I certainly have enjoyed corresponding with you. I too wish that I lived closer to Omaha and that we could share conversations in person.

Well, here goes! I have decided to go ahead with my search. I have enclosed a copy of a letter I received from the State of Nebraska that I was instructed to supply to you. At the same time that I originally contacted NCHS, I also requested a copy of my birth certificate, as I did not have a copy. At that time I asked about my original birth certificate and received the very same form that you sent with your last letter. I had mailed in a completed form with fee to them at the same time I wrote you last. Your letter and the State of Nebraska's came just one day apart. I did feel that there was a "good omen" quality to that. I have extensively considered my feelings and how this action may affect others. I have discussed all of this with several people close to me, including the counselor I have been seeing for the past year, and I have decided as you wisely put it, "to trust my own feelings." I want to make the contact. That's it, plain and simply put and felt.

I am not certain what happens next, but I have also enclosed my letter to my birth mother and hope that is appropriate. I know you will let me know if I have skipped a step.

I am nervous, excited, hopeful, worried and happy. I believe that is exactly what I should be.

I will wait to hear from you and, as always, I sincerely appreciate all of your thoughts and assistance.

Thank you.

Sincerely,

Nancy Feldman

Becky's Note: *As mandated by law, the agency's role is to be an intermediary for the adopted person. Nancy requested a search for her birth mother and the process began.*

The agency's policy has been to ask the adopted person to write a letter to the birth relative being sought. The reasons for requesting a letter are to help the searcher collect and process his or her thoughts about contacting a real person. It also provides the caseworker an instrument to offer the person being sought as an introduction instead of immediate direct contact. The shock of being contacted after many years can be considerable, and a letter is a way to ease into the situation.

After locating someone, the caseworker would offer the searcher's letter and ask the birth parent to consider answering the letter. This process is one that gives people time to reflect and not act in an impulsive manner. Nancy wrote a remarkable letter.

June 27, 1994

To the woman who gave me life:

Why now after all of this time?

In April of this year, I requested a family medical background on myself from the Nebraska Children's Home Society as I hoped it would help in understanding and possibly treating some medical maladies that I have been experiencing. I discovered then that the story I had been told that my mother had died shortly after my birth was untrue. It was indeed a startling revelation. I had believed up to that day that my birth father had given me up for adoption. I again contacted the NCHS and asked if I could be privy to more background information. Without jeopardizing the confidentiality of your identity, I was provided an extensive background that told of an incredible woman and her family. I was in awe.

After extensive consideration and realizing that there are risks involved, I have decided to write to you through the NCHS. And this is what I want to tell you: Thank you for giving me life. My birth altered your life at that time, I know. It took a tremendous amount of courage to go through our pregnancy. I want you to know that I admire you for that and will honor the existence of you. You then gave me up for adoption to an agency that utilized all the extensive background you had provided and then matched me perfectly. Without knowing, you gifted two strangers with a child they so desperately had wanted. I was a happy child raised by two adoring parents. I am a contented adult. I have a child, 21 years of age, a rather wild, young man, most certainly an artist. Like his mother, he is a lover of the written word and collects poetry. I think that is even more special now, as I know that is what you did.

You and I are in two different worlds. My being might be an unwanted intrusion into yours and I want you to know that I do not expect and will not demand anything from you. But after learning that you had not perished after my birth and having received my amazing background, I just had to extend these words out to you. It became important to me to be able to tell you how much I appreciated what you did for me and tell you that I grew up happy and loved. I want you to know that I will not write this same letter to my birth father. It was your wish that he not know of my birth and I will continue to honor that wish. I would be guilty of deceit if I did not admit to a desire to receive more information about you and your background.

I have also fantasized about actually meeting you, but I am adamant about not being a burden suddenly thrust into your life. I feel very protective of you. If you wish to let our contact end with this letter, I will be accepting of that. However, if you wish to contact me, I would be pleased to hear from you. As a woman and a mother, I could not resist this opportunity to express my feelings to you and to let you know that I honor you.

Sincerely,

Nancy Elaine Feldman

Becky's Note: *Nancy wrote a beautiful letter full of care and respect. These letters are not easy to write. Telling about yourself to a stranger in writing is hard enough but harder still with all of the ramifications of emotional involvement. Some people simply write a short description of themselves, their jobs, family, and other details. Writing the letter often helps the writer to clarify his or her thinking as well as emotions. It also serves as a commitment to reaching out to a birth relative.*

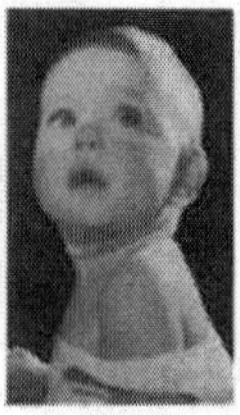

CHARTERED 1893

Nebraska Children's Home Society

3549 Fontenelle Boulevard — Omana, Nebraska 68104
(402) 451-0787 — FAX (402) 451-0360

A Private Non-sectarian Agency Providing Adoption Services • Temporary Foster Care • Services to Single Pregnant Women • Emergency Shelter Care

July 18, 1994

Dear Nancy,

I received your letter and the copy of the letter from the Bureau of Vital Statistics. Thanks.

We will begin a search for your birth mother. There is no way of knowing how long it may be, but I'll certainly be in touch as soon as I know something.

Thanks.

Sincerely,

Nebraska Children's Home Society

Rebecca Crofoot

Caseworker

This Is Really Happening

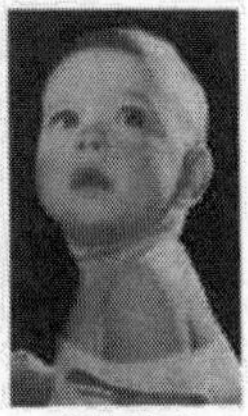

CHARTERED 1893

Nebraska Children's Home Society

3549 Fontenelle Boulevard — Omana, Nebraska 68104
(402) 451-0787 — FAX (402) 451-0360

A Private Non-sectarian Agency Providing Adoption Services • Temporary Foster Care • Services to Single Pregnant Women • Emergency Shelter Care

December 12, 1994

Dear Nancy:

I wanted to drop you a note to let you know that I think I have located your birth mother. I am writing to her today. I know nothing about her other than her married name and address so don't know what to expect.

I'll let you know when I know more!
Nebraska Children's Home Society
Rebecca Crofoot
Caseworker

Becky's Note: *The agency has information about the birth mother such as birth date and place and full name. However, her married name would not be available unless she had been in contact with the agency through the years to make her whereabouts known. The vast majority of the older birth mothers have not done that. Search engines like Ancestry.com are often used as well as public records.*

Oh, oh, this is really happening!

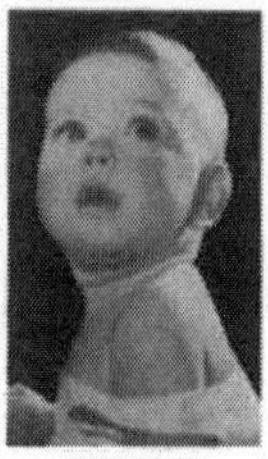

CHARTERED 1893

Nebraska Children's Home Society

3549 Fontenelle Boulevard — Omana, Nebraska 68104
(402) 451-0787 — FAX (402) 451-0360

A Private Non-sectarian Agency Providing Adoption Services • Temporary Foster Care • Services to Single Pregnant Women • Emergency Shelter Care

January 23, 1995

Dear Nancy:

I finally have talked with your birth mother. She had written a long sad letter after the Holidays about the circumstances of your birth, most of which we knew. She said she would call and then we could talk. She called on the 20th and we had a long conversation.

She was pleasant and not angry. She obviously had put a great deal of thought in all this and we talked a long time. The conclusion, though, was that she will do nothing and she doesn't want to reopen the past. She said she would keep my letter in case she ever felt differently. I told her what her rights were and I suggested various options of limited contact with you. She continued to say that it is best left alone. She specifically wanted you to know that it was "done out of love." She wished you health and happiness always.

I told her as much as I could about you and she was interested but did not ask any questions. She has had a good life. She seemed to have always felt that she made a good plan for you and she had made her peace with that, years ago.

She said that she is in her mid-70s and in very good health. She's quite sharp. According to her, all of her ancestors were healthy people who "died of old age." She had a sister who died of the flu, which somehow infected her heart. I tried to connect that with mitral valve prolapse but she didn't think so. She knew nothing of the birth father's family medical history.

No one now living knows about this but she decided that she would tell her husband. He had opened my letter to her but had not said anything about it. She was not anxious about telling him and felt sure that it would not upset him. She did say that they have children and grandchildren located near them.

She talked at great length about what a difficult time this was in her life. There was no self-pity in her conversation but it was obvious how painful it had all been. However, I felt that she has long ago resolved her feelings and has handled it well.

She firmly believed (and still does) that she did the right thing and hearing about your life only reaffirmed her belief.

As we ended the conversation she said again that she wanted me to tell you that she "always loved you."

I know that this is disappointing to you but I think there's a good chance she may reconsider at some point. Let's hope!

Sincerely,
Nebraska Children's Home Society
Rebecca Crofoot
Caseworker

I was astounded. She's out there somewhere. She got married, had kids, and they have kids. She's happy. I wanted her to be. I did hope that she would want some contact, but I believe I knew all along that she couldn't do it. It was something that happened long ago. She was hurt, but she made the best of it. I cried, but not long and hard. I kept thinking how much I had learned and grown in this search. It was a lot more than I ever expected. I had wanted her to know that I was safe and loved. I had accomplished that by not turning her world upside down. Michael read the letter and said, "Maybe she'll change her mind."

We went to the home of our friends Linda and Bill for a birthday dinner for me. I walked in the door, we hugged like we always do, and she said, "What's wrong?"

I said, "Not wrong, just that I got an answer." She gasped and I handed her the letter. I remember not being able to speak. She read the letter and at the end, she started crying, saying, "I don't know why I am crying, but I am thinking that this is sad. Are you sad?"

"Yes. But I understand."

And Linda said, "I know you do."

The next day at work, my birthday, I couldn't tell my friend Carol on the phone what the letter said. Instead I met her outside by the library. I was smoking (which I wasn't supposed to be doing) and I said, "My mom doesn't want to meet me," and then I started crying hard and Carol was hugging me and saying, "It's okay, it's okay. Think of all you learned. Let me read it."

And she read it and said, "She may change her mind."

But we both knew that she wouldn't, and we both understood why. Soon I was relieved because I wasn't going to have to explain anything to my parents. No deception as to why I was going somewhere. And no worry that my mom, in fragile mental health even then, would think I was looking for my "real" mom. I had been done a favor.

Becky's Note: *Nancy's reactions to her birth mother's refusal for contact were normal. Although the outcome was definitely disappointing, Nancy now knew more than she had previously known. There also remained the possibility that the birth mother might change her mind in the future.*

January 31, 1995

Ms. Rebecca Crofoot
Nebraska Children's Home Society
Dear Rebecca:

Your letter arrived on January 25th and made a perfect birthday gift for me. My birthday was January 26th, and it was a day of distinction in that it is the first time in 46 years that I knew exactly my birth time and that I had the true story of my background—all thanks to you and NCHS.

I am disappointed only in that the adventure that you and I began last April is now at its conclusion. You have been a wonderful advocate for me and have collected more information and details than I ever dreamed possible. Just think—this all started with one physician encouraging me to try to collect my medical background. I will miss our correspondence relationship. You helped me grow, truly you did. I most certainly came out of this experience with more than I went into it. My husband is grateful to you as well in that my expanded family medical history is good news: my ancestors lived long lives!

I was so relieved that my birth mother was in good health, had experienced a good life, had married and had children. I wanted her to have had a good, positive life with all the special dimensions that loving someone and having children provides. In addition, it was very important to me to hear that my intrusion had not caused or would not create a problem for her.

My goal was to reach out to her and let her know that her decision had been for the best and that I was fine. More detail, even contact, would have been welcomed on my part, but I never expected it to happen. I was not surprised that she preferred not to open the past. Somehow I just knew. It must have been a very difficult time for her and no one has the right to attempt to force someone to go through that again. I was moved to tears when I read "… she wanted me to tell you that she 'always loved you.'" I felt so badly that until last April I never knew of her existence, let alone her love. Just knowing that provides me with a very special feeling and assurance that will carry me throughout the rest of my life. What I have received is enough.

I've gone through all my correspondence with you and it seems like I have spent a lot of time thanking you, but it was all sincere and I am going to do it again. Thank you for your time, consideration and terrific sleuthing. You made it all happen for me and I do sincerely appreciate it.

It appears that a transfer move for my husband and I will happen by this coming summer. We will probably be settled in Portland, Oregon, by 4th of July. Leaving California after so many years is rather unsettling, but I am excited about Portland and the opportunity to experience seasons again. I will let you and NCHS know of my new address just in case.

I hope that all is well with you. I know that you will continue your very fine work with those who

First trip to Grandpa Arthur and Grandma Anna McGann's farm, near Columbus, Nebraska, Spring 1949.

Here's my baby!
Mom and me, March 1949.

One happy momma with her baby in Spring 1949.

My parents' first and only grandchild, June 1973, my parents' home in Rancho Palos Verdes, California.
From left: Lucille Kacirek, Nancy Kacirek Cole, George Kacirek holding Forrest Grail Cole.

require your assistance. I will never forget you and your extreme kindness to me.

Go well.

Sincerely,

Nancy Feldman

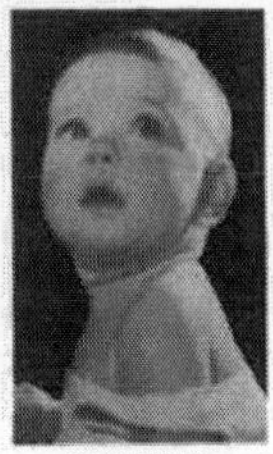

CHARTERED 1893

Nebraska Children's Home Society

3549 Fontenelle Boulevard — Omana, Nebraska 68104
(402) 451-0787 — FAX (402) 451-0360

A Private Non-sectarian Agency Providing Adoption Services • Temporary Foster Care • Services to Single Pregnant Women • Emergency Shelter Care

February 16, 1995

Dear Nancy:

Thank you for your lovely letter. I so wish we could have done more but I'm always certain there's a reason for everything. I just wish that I knew what it was more often!

I'm sure that it is a relief to know that she is living and in good health. I also hope that it will give her more peace of mind knowing a little about you. It remains to be seen if she decides that she would like to know more.

Your acceptance of her decision was gracious and loving just as her words were. The expression of your feelings was beautiful and I wish I could share it with her. It tells a great deal about you and also how your parents handled the subject of adoption. I'm so glad that you can be somewhat at peace with her decision for your sake. But, also it's important because she is content with the decision she made years ago and that's wonderful to know.

I'm glad this has been a good experience for you. Please keep in touch. Maybe you'll get to Omaha someday!

Sincerely,
Nebraska Children's Home Society
Rebecca Crofoot
Caseworker

Becky's Note: *Nancy's letter was not sent to her birth mother although parts were read to her on the phone. She did not want to receive any further mail. Her strong refusal for any contact with Nancy was an indication of the intensity of her emotions at this point. In a subsequent phone conversation at a later date, she was more calm although no less determined. We were able to have a reasonable conversation, nevertheless.*

Birth parents who have experienced an inquiry about the past display a broad range of emotions from anger to overwhelming joy. A minority (usually older women) refuse contact with many expressing fear that their subsequent children will think less of them if they knew of their mother's secret. They often feel a strong sense of betrayal by the agency. Reassurances that they will not be approached by the agency again because of Nebraska law are hardly enough to console them.

Now What? Life Intervenes

Michael and I had started talking about living somewhere besides L.A. after we saw Steve Martin's movie *Roxanne* in 1987. On the screen, I fell in love with the small town of Nelson, Washington, the setting of the movie. It was filled with wonderful, old Victorian-type houses and a downtown of old buildings. However, Nelson, Washington, doesn't exist, but Nelson, British Columbia, Canada, does.

Michael was a Vietnam vet and I was a protestor against the war. Michael had a low draft number and enlisted in the Navy to avoid going to Vietnam. Instead he got two tours, one in country. He came home disillusioned, not wanting to discuss anything about the war. He joined a motorcycle club, not as exciting or dangerous as the Angels, but I've seen the pictures, and he looked pretty scary.

By the time we met, he had tamed down considerably, and my protest signs had been replaced by a baby backpack. Still, we both agreed, the Vietnam War was a mistake. Going to Canada sounded tempting to two old peaceniks, but complicated. We started dreaming anyway about where we could go once retirement age came around in the early 2000s. Then in 1991, Michael was downsized from Wang, and our biggest reason for staying in L.A. for secure employment for Michael was gone.

For a few years, he went through a series of computer sales jobs that entailed six months employed, six months on unemployment. We had become disillusioned even with our seemingly safe South Bay life due to random, violent crimes prevalent to Los Angeles. Shootings had become commonplace, and we had almost completely stopped going out at night, even in our community where we had felt safe before. We started talking about not waiting for retirement to leave L.A.

A point for staying would be our parents. Both sets of our parents were alive and apparently healthy, but they were in those sunset years. Mine were in the Los Angeles area, and Michael's were a five-hour car ride away in Arizona.

A point for going was the home we had purchased in 1988 at 13 percent interest on the mortgage. We were continually feeling the bite of making certain that the house payment was made. Once during an unemployment time, Michael approached our bank and asked if we could make a partial payment, to which he was told, "If you make a partial payment, we will start foreclosure immediately." Not the warm fuzzy-feeling bank we were hoping for.

For our dream life, we decided we would stay on the West Coast. Michael agreed to look at Denver because of the great skiing, but he refused to consider the Midwest, even though the housing prices were so much lower, as he said, "I never want to be that cold again." Having grown up in Minnesota, he knew what he was talking about.

We knew for both of us to be employed, we would have to rule out small towns. So goodbye Nelson, Washington! Michael needed a larger city for sales work, and I needed a large medical center, like the one where I was working in L.A.

So we started looking for that perfect place. We had a standing invitation from former work friends of Michael's to visit Portland, and so we took up Merrill and Noveta's gracious invitation in February 1991. We arrived to experience one of Portland's rare snowstorms. They kept telling us that the city was shut down and they were both off work.

Merrill greeted us with "Welcome to the Yukon, Jack!" They took us to their home for "tubing" behind their car on country roads, and by 10:30 in the morning we were sitting in the hot tub, drinking coffee and Kahlua. We were sitting there thinking, *Is this magical or what?* Our friends drove us to the beach and the mountains and we were enchanted.

But this was a big decision, and we felt we needed to check other cities. So we came back in the summer of 1993. This time we spent one week in Portland and one in Seattle. Portland was again magical. Our friends lent us a car for the journey north. We loved West Seattle; we could sense the small town feel with the benefits of being attached to a large city. We did a "fake" commute from West Seattle to the University of Washington Medical Center in mid-day traffic. It took over an hour.

Our final conclusion was that Seattle was L.A. with trees and ferries. But again so tempting were those low real estate prices when compared to L.A. During this two-week fact-finding mission, we had noted to our chagrin that the Pacific Northwest did not appreciate the transplant Californians who had moved up with "bags of money" and who had "jacked the price of real estate up." At one party we were taken to, we heard horror stories of transplant mistreatment (windshields bashed, tow truck refusals) and were even told by one party guest, "Don't come up here; we don't want you!"

We returned to L.A. and to our jobs and wondered where we could go where we would be welcome. This brought us to Denver in September 1994, but our prime destination was Boulder. Yes, I'll admit it. It had the Nelson look to it. But we were so out of our league. Salaries were low (one secretarial job with a minimum wage salary said "Must have own car.") and housing was *high*.

We spent Sunday in Denver going to open houses for rentals and we couldn't even afford those. So we went to Golden to see the Coors Brewery, which, of course, was closed. We stopped at Red Rocks amphitheater and were amazed at it, and then it was late Sunday night and we were back on the plane to go home to California.

Our spirits were low as we reviewed the long weekend that had started with such hopes. There seemed to be few jobs with living wages and housing prices were just as high as L.A. And we were shocked how flat the area was. Denver is the "Mile High City," but one forgets about the high plateaus that make up Colorado. It is the Rocky Mountain State, but there is a lot of non-mountainous land as well. Dejected, Michael said, "What are we going to do?"

My reply was, "It's Portland, and we go in a year!"

Upon our return home, I called our Portland friends with the query, "Are housing prices still reasonable?" The answer was positive, and I told them, "Look for us in the summer of 1995."

And we made good on our promise. Michael found a sales job before the move, and I found medical secretary employment at the School of Medicine shortly after we arrived. We looked at everything with wonder. It had been decades since either one of us had experienced fall. We spent two years exploring our new town and area. In fact, our friends claimed that we had seen more than they. We truly loved our new life.

At work, I was suddenly meeting so many people who had been adopted. I have always believed that everyone has a story and they are all worth hearing. So I spent a lot of time with these adoptees, sharing stories. Most felt that I should search further for my birth mother and birth father. I was still hesitant about doing this. I felt I had gained more information and growth than I ever thought was possible. And I kept going back to my birth mother's request for no contact. And then it was Christmas of 1997, and I wondered how Becky was doing.

[The following message was hand written in our Christmas card, 1997.]

Dear Rebecca:

The Christmas holidays are most certainly a time for reflection; and in that tone, I have been recalling

Alleluia, Christmas card, 1997.

our nine months of correspondence regarding my feelings toward adoption and my subsequent desire to reach out to my birth mother and tell her she had nothing to worry about me. You were indeed a true counselor and friend to me during that time, and I continue to appreciate what you gave to me.

Since in Oregon, I have met several adopted individuals. Their feelings toward this are as varied as the color spectrum. The conversations are always stimulating and moving. I have just discovered that another friend is adopted. She is on the brink of starting a search. I want her to read my file of letters from you first. I am certain she will get valuable insight from your words.

Best wishes to you.

Nancy Kacirek Feldman

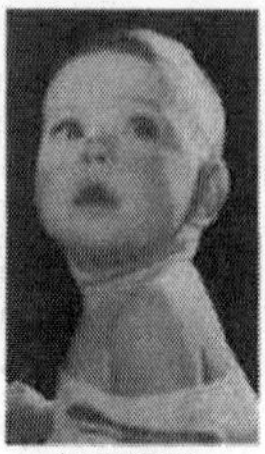

CHARTERED 1893

Nebraska Children's Home Society

3549 Fontenelle Boulevard — Omana, Nebraska 68104
(402) 451-0787 — FAX (402) 451-0360

A Private Non-sectarian Agency Providing Adoption Services • Temporary Foster Care • Services to Single Pregnant Women • Emergency Shelter Care

January 7, 1998

Dear Nancy,

It was lovely to hear from you and also that your feelings about your birth mother are still changing and evolving. It truly does help to talk to other people and the support works both ways. I'm glad you are sharing and thinking out loud with others.

I keep hoping that your birth mother might have a change of heart but I'm sure the chances are quite slim. Knowing that you did reach out to her, as you said, must give her some peace of mind. You actually were able to do what you set out to do. However, it certainly would have been nice if it had resulted in more!

I hope all is well with you and yours. Our best to you for 1998, and thank for your kind words.

Sincerely,
Nebraska Children's Home Society
Rebecca Crofoot
Caseworker

As long as I can remember, I knew that I was adopted and loved. My first memories—it's like coming up from deep water, right?—are from Kansas City, Kansas. There were big roses on the wallpaper in my bedroom and cut outs of Hey, Diddle, Diddle, the Cat and the Fiddle. I loved looking at those characters. I got excited seeing any animal and I called all of them, "Bobbins."

My dad had gone to work for Mobil Oil, Omaha, in about 1947, as a chemist. The plant manager, Mr. Brown, aka Brownie, took a liking to my dad and mom and coaxed him into plant operations.

The first house that my parents stopped at after getting me was the Brown's. I always believed the Browns were part of our family and always called them Brownie and Audrey. When Mr. Brown was transferred to Kansas City, he took my dad with him. So we started in Omaha and then moved to Shawnee Mission, Kansas, We were transferred back to Omaha when I turned five, and my dad became the Mobil plant manager.

We lived in two different houses in the Minne Lusa area, and I attended grades kindergarten through fifth at Minne Lusa School. In the summer of 1960, while I was watching the Democratic Convention (only because my mom had said not to change the channel), my dad walked in, saying, "Well, Nancy, how would you like to move to Chicago?" Mobil was again transferring us.

I was crazy about horses, and my parents provided me with yearly riding lessons and riding sessions at Hillside Stables in Omaha. I had begged for a horse and had been told that if I was responsible, got good grades and all of those yardsticks parents put up there, I could get a horse when I was thirteen.

With the move, my folks decided to let my greatest dream come true. With the help of the Wolff brothers who owned Hillside Stables, they bought and trailered King from Omaha to a stable in Hinsdale, Illinois. We lived in nearby LaGrange. My grandfather had been living with us since my grandmother's death three years before, and so the four of us plus King moved to the Chicago area.

I loved my horse and the lush forest preserves with miles and miles of riding trails that had been designed years before by what must have been wonderful people. In 1964, before the political conventions could start, my dad accepted his last transfer with Mobil Oil. California. He used to say that it was every smart Mobil employee's dream to be transferred to California.

My dad crossed the state line and never looked back or expressed a desire to see snow. He embraced L.A. life. No more shoveling snow, no more cars stuck in the snow, no more snow. In Chicago, he had transitioned into marketing from plant work, so he became the regional safety director for the West Coast. He loved his job and it showed.

My mom made the most of every move. She had to leave family behind (but many were starting to move around the country as much as we were), but she never lost touch. She called and she visited. And she had me. She set great store in my company. And we talked and we talked and we talked. She thought everything I said was clever and that I was "very mechanical." Disclaimer: There were plenty of clashes and my brilliance as a mechanic was based on my ability to stop the TV from vertically rotating.

Above all, I was adored and I knew it. I never felt a hunger for food, shelter, clothing, or, most importantly, love. I would say that I was tolerably spoiled. I was indulged, but I could not command receipt of any whimsical desire. But I could talk about anything openly and honestly.

The years were busy with jobs, many adventures, and many trips to Los Angeles for me as my mother's health deteriorated. My father felt my move to Portland had been a defection. I encouraged him to get assistance in caring for my mom, but he refused to do this, saying each time I suggested that, "You should be here to help me with your mother."

It took me a long time to realize that with her gradual decline into dementia due to the strokes, he was losing her a little bit every day. Michael's mother was also experiencing some dementia-like difficulties, but Michael's father was adamant that it was not Alzheimer's.

We both felt that our mothers' health would cause them to die first. We did not want to be unprepared to find care and housing for our fathers at our mothers' funerals. So we found a company that was a valuable resource. In fact, they were called Resource Connectors. Through them and the facilities that we visited, we discovered that Portland had affordable elder care. We felt with our list of ten excellent places that ranged from senior living to skilled nursing care, we were ready.

And then our twenty-seven-year-old son became ill. This we weren't prepared for. He had passed out six times in less than a week. Once of these spells occurred while he was in the shower. He was admitted to the University Hospital in Salt Lake City, and we went there immediately.

Through testing it was determined that his heart was stopping during these "attacks." A pacemaker was recommended. He had the distinction of having the same pacemaker installed as his Grandfather Kacirek, my dad. He was discharged and went back to school at the University of Utah, Salt Lake City, and worked for his uncle, installing floors, but was ordered not to drive for six months. Forrest had moved there to be near his biological father after following The Grateful Dead for two years.

I went home to Portland, and I know that I went through the mechanics of life—eating, drinking, working, going out with friends, but I was constantly going over what had happened to Forrest in my head. *How had this happened? What medical problem had I missed while he was growing up? What had his doctors missed? What is this going to mean in the future?*

No one knows the cause. They're not certain what it was in the first place, just that he needed a pacemaker. But he did get better and stronger and then it was New Year's Eve and everyone was concerned about Y2K. Michael was busy with finding jobs for computer personnel to write new code for Y2K. There was a riot in downtown Portland that New Year's Eve, which shocked everyone. Rioting was so against the mellowness of Portland. We stayed home. Our shutdown came two days into the New Year.

Michael's dad called to say that his mother had collapsed and had been taken by ambulance to the hospital. His dad didn't know why she had collapsed, she just had. So Michael called his mother's doctor who explained that quite often the Alzheimer patient experiences decreases in appetite as the cluster in the brain grows. "That's what happened with your mom. The messages didn't get through to the brain, so she stopped eating. She was quite malnourished."

Although on the phone, the physician could tell that Michael was in shock.

"Your dad didn't tell you that she had Alzheimer's, did he?"

"No, he always said that she just had some minor strokes. Have you been treating her for very long?" Michael asked.

"It's been three years now. I'm sorry you didn't know. Your father's behavior is quite typical of the Alzheimer's spouse. If he admitted she had Alzheimer's, he would have known that improvement would have been impossible. With a stroke, he had hopes that she would return to what she was. I'm sorry to be the one to tell you. I know this is tough. And I'm sorry that I have to be the one to tell you that she won't be getting better and she will not be able to go home. She will have to be in a secured Alzheimer's facility from now on. And the only one in the area is forty-five minutes from here."

And so our research was used to the fullest. From March through August 2000, we handled the process that relocated Michael's parents to Portland. His father went into a senior apartment setting where he could have his dog. Michael's mom went into a secure Alzheimer's facility that was brand new and very homey feeling. Michael's dad was so grateful to have things taken care of, and he enjoyed his life in Portland.

In September 2000, my mother's doctor finally insisted that she be admitted for skilled nursing care. She had reached the point where she could chew but not swallow, and she could not walk. Knowing that I would be traveling to L.A. on many weekends, I quit my job in order to search for one that would only be four days a week. I went down to Los Angeles in February 2001 for a four-day visit.

My father had fallen just before I got there. He ended up in the hospital and subsequently in an extended care facility. At that time he stated that he wanted the two of them to move to Portland where I could help them. Again, the necessary information was available exactly when I needed it. My four-day weekend turned into four months in L.A. taking care of everything for my dad and listing his house for sale.

Having promised my father that I would stay in L.A., at his house, until it sold, I was just finishing my morning shower when the phone rang. I had established a rigid routine for myself during those four months. I would leave the west-facing curtain open in my bedroom. The sun would wake me up, and I would get up and walk for an hour in my parents' hilly neighborhood. Upon my return to the house, I would shower and then drive to the rehabilitation facility where both of my parents were.

My mom was in the nursing home part and my dad was in the rehab part recovering from a big-time fall. His chronic obstructive pulmonary disease (COPD/emphysema/asthma) plagued him as well. I would visit with them both and then do any errands that my dad wanted me to. I filled the rest of my day with chores and a lot of movies.

The phone rang and my life as a daughter changed forever. My dad told me that mom had aspirated and had been taken to the hospital emergency room, one block from the rehab center. I remembered thinking, but not saying, *How could she have aspirated? She's being fed by a G-tube?*

I said, "Will she come back from this?"

He replied, "I don't know, Nance, but I think you had better get down there. I can't go."

I told him something like "I'm on my way." I remember looking in the mirror and thinking that I had better do something more with my hair; otherwise, she might have a fit. She had been mentally in the shadows for so long and her body had been ravaged by mini-strokes for years. So often I had come from Portland to visit and seen her just barely existing, and no matter what, the headaches would still come and I felt so badly for her and used to think, *Oh, little bird, fly away from all of this. Fly away.* And now here we were.

As my mom always hated pants, particularly jeans, I wore a dress. I considered a hat too, but decided against it as I knew I would probably have to find a place to put it down. And off I went.

Once at the ER and after identifying who I was, I was immediately taken to her gurney. The ER was divided with curtains, and as these were constantly being pulled back and forth, I could see other patients and they could see us. Her eyes were closed and she was gasping for breath. The doctor came in right away, announced that he knew there was a DNR (do not resuscitate) order and that he did not think that she would last another hour.

I thought, *Oh, no, you're wrong there. My mom was never on time and she won't die on anyone's timetable.* I smiled inside, but it was not a big smile. She struggled so, and the doctor, a kind man, expressed his sympathy for her struggle. He got some type of relaxant, and it made a small difference. Her hands laid on the gurney next to her. I picked her right hand up, it was warm, but lifeless. I held it anyway and I talked to her, and rubbed her hand, massaged it and continued to talk.

I told her that she may not have been at my birth, but she would be my mother for all time. The hours went by, patients came and went, the curtains got parted, people saw my mom and me and everyone looked alarmed.

One man asked, "What's wrong with her?" I couldn't answer him; I just looked back at my mom. At 4:00 p.m., the doctor returned, saying he was surprised that she had lasted this long (and I was thinking, *Told you.*), and that he thought she should be transferred across town to her Kaiser hospital. I was raised by a nurse and graduate pharmacist to accept what doctors said and not to question.

And yet, Lucille and George's daughter looked at that kind man and said, "You and I both know that my mom is not getting better and if you put her in an ambulance, she's going to die on the way there. Why not send her back to her room one block away to the nursing home? That's been her home for the last six months. Let her die there."

To which he said, "I think that is a much better idea."

I walked back to the nursing home and reached Mom's room just as the paramedics had lifted her into her bed. She died right then. And the pain left her face, and I found myself, saying, "Look at you, look at you, Mama, you're free."

And I think about her almost every day because I have made certain that there is something in every room of my house that if it wasn't hers, it is something she would have had or liked. And I have tried to be the kind of mother and woman she was, so that I can make a difference in the lives of those who love or know me.

Whale watching. From the left: My husband's, Michael Feldman, back, me hugging my mom, Lucille Kacirek, with grandson, Forrest Cole in jacket.

That August, Michael's mother, at age seventy-eight, passed away. Although we knew that they had been very ill, it was so hard to believe that both of our mothers were gone. Michael's father went into a depression that he would never come out of. He went through several medical facilities during the last seven months of his life—VA skilled nursing, VA hospital, university hospital, and several nursing homes.

My dad moved to Portland in October 2001. He lived in an assisted living apartment just five minutes away from us. He made the best of his new surroundings. It was sad that he only got to see Michael's dad once. In March 2002, Michael's dad died. It was just one day short of the year anniversary of my mother's death.

Smiling Through My Tears

During the years of 1999 to 2002, I would satisfy my curiosity by checking the Internet. I wanted to know more about my birth mother and her family without bothering her. I would type in the name Carroll and go through all the Midwestern states. I tried looking at the Social Security death records, trying to find my maternal birth grandfather's death, but Carroll is not an unusual name, and I was looking in a lot of states. The end result was always frustration.

I noted some of the search boards where messages were placed, but I didn't want to do that. There was a book entitled *Women in the Military, World War II,* but I decided not to do anything. The only thing I ever got was eyestrain and a headache. In the end, I gave up.

And then I volunteered for a study about iron overload.

January 6, 2003

Ms. Rebecca Crofoot
Caseworker
Nebraska Children's Home Society

Dear Rebecca:

In May 1994, you and I began a relationship through the mail that provided me with a great deal of growth as an adopted child and woman. I receive the NCHS publication, Home Talk, and am delighted to find you mentioned in almost every issue. You continue to have many positive interactions and activities with the folks of your community. Most recently, a Home Talk described a wonderful caseworker named Rebecca in a placement story. Of course, it was no surprise to learn at the end of the article that the caseworker was you.

As I had appreciated our correspondence in 1994–1995, I had thought to write you several times since Oregon passed legislation to open adoptive birth certificates, curious to know what you might think of it. You possibly were aware of the media impact this new law had in that it was opposed and kept from going into effect for over a year. I believe that the compromise reached on this issue was a fair one. Individuals wishing not to have contact from the children they have given up may leave a note attached to the birth certificate stating this. Only five states in the US have adopted this measure. Is there any such movement in Nebraska? I am just curious.

I cannot deny that I still have continued to be curious about my background. I do wish there was a way that I could obtain information without jeopardizing my birth mother's identity or privacy or that of her family. Of course, everyone is searching on the Internet these days, but it is not my intent to seek out family members. I promised that I would not do that, and I intend to adhere to that promise.

In September 2000, my mother, with health ravaged by numerous strokes, was admitted into a nursing facility for first NG tube feeding and then G-tube feeding. She had been lovingly cared for by my dad prior to that and his efforts nearly cost him his health and life.

In February 2001, I went for a four-day visit and ended up staying for four months as my dad collapsed and had to be hospitalized. He decided that he no longer wanted to stay in the Los Angeles area and that he wanted to now move my mom and himself to Portland. My husband and I had started a search two years before, recognizing that we needed to make some plans for our parents beforehand. With both parents in facilities, it was up to me to get the house ready for sale and go through everything that both my parents and their parents had collected. I found a wonderful wealth of pictures, letters, documents, … many of which I have shared with other relatives (near and distant) and even some historical societies of Columbus, Nebraska.

I have not started the Omaha archives section yet, but that's this winter's project. And then on March 22, 2001, the world drastically changed for me forever in that my mother aspirated on that morning and passed from this world late that afternoon. I spent the afternoon with her, holding her hand. She never regained consciousness, but that was of little matter to me. I remember thinking, "You may not have been there when I was ushered into this world, but we were together for my whole life and I will stay with you until you must leave. You are my mother for all time." I was devastated, but I will carry on because that is the way that my mother raised me.

As I continued to pack up my parent's home, I discovered the letter they received in 1950 from NCHS. A letter that stated the adoption papers could be filed. I was theirs. I remembered when I first saw it in 1970, and was so surprised that I was listed as Baby Girl Carroll, and when I asked my mom why she had never told me that she knew my last name, she said, "I don't even remember that being mentioned! I was so elated that the waiting was finally over! No one was going to take you away. You were mine!"

This past summer I participated in a study for Hemochromatosis and Iron Overload at Kaiser Permanente here in Portland. I did recall a comment made several years ago from my physician, saying, "You do seem to have a high concentration of iron in your body," and so I thought it a good idea to volunteer. The results are that I have the HFE C282Y genotype homozygote. This means I inherited both "positive" genes from my biological parents. The good news? I am just slightly above the normal range and will probably not require "blood letting" for some time.

I do want my son, Forrest, to have his blood tested as soon as possible now that he has returned from school in Spain. I wondered if iron overload contributed in his heart problem four years ago that required the installation of a pacemaker. Women with this condition lose extra iron every month with their menses, but obviously males do not have that benefit. (Imagine, menstruation being considered a benefit?)

During the testing procedure, I met with several individuals, including a genetic counselor. I explained my adoptive status, and asked her about the need to contact my birth mother with regards to this condition for her children. I told her that my birth mother did not desire contact with me, but the counselor thought she might also appreciate knowing this. So, it is a dilemma, isn't it? Early detection could mean a big difference, but I would not want my birth mother to think that I am blaming her for anything, because simply, I am not. If knowing about this and recommending blood tests for her children spared them any future health problems, I would be pleased to know that I have done something good. But I also realize that her children do not draw from the same gene pool as I did, and genetic possibilities are diverse. So, remembering your sage advice during our adventure, I decided to write you about this, and once again, seek your advice about what to do. I know that you will make the right decision.

For your review, I have enclosed a copy of my lab results and an explanation letter that cites several Internet sites. In the 1980s I had to deal with mitral valve prolapse (which resolved in the 1990s), in the 1990s I had several years of problems with interstitial cystitis. Fortunately, since my move to Oregon in 1995, the IC has almost been non-existent. So with the turn of the millennium, I guess it's time for another "designer" medical condition for me. Hardy, har har!

I hope that you and your family are well. Again, I want you to know that I hold you in the highest regard and always will.

With best wishes,
Nancy Kacirek Feldman
Portland, OR

Becky's Note: *The movement in Oregon to open adoption files has continued in other states. Every adopted person can benefit by knowing more about their history and birth relatives. More openness is good except for those who feel that they have been betrayed by agencies who promised that their secret would* *never be revealed, as illustrated here. Subsequent generations cannot imagine the secrecy, let alone the stigma unwed mothers felt in the past.*

In the past unplanned pregnancies were treated with great shame. Pregnant women were sent away from their home communities to relatives or a maternity home under the guise of going to school or to help a relative. Many maternity homes required the pregnant women to feed and care for their babies for several months until a doctor would determine that they were healthy enough to be placed for adoption. Others never saw their child and and papers were signed relinquishing their parental rights, making their decision final.

The birth mother understood that the adoption was closed, and she was expected to go on with her life forgetting about the child. Some states had strict laws governing the secrecy, but society's attitude toward secrecy was prevalent everywhere. Laws and practices were established to protect the adoptive parents from the birth mother, but there was also a strong feeling that the identity of the birth mother also was to be protected.

By contrast, today's adoptions, especially through agencies, are open with the birth parent(s) making an adoption plan rather than feeling that society is forcing them to "give up" their child. Birth parent(s) often meet the adoptive parents before the birth of the child and go on to have a lifetime relationship with the adoptive family.

nebraska children's home society

3549 Fontenelle Blvd.
Omaha, NE 68104
(402)451-0787
fax:(402)451-0360
www.nchs.org

The Nebraska Children's Home Society provides safe and loving care to children of all ages.

OFFICES
Fremont • Gothenburg
Grand Island • Kearney
Lincoln • Norfolk
North Platte • Omaha
Scottsbluff

02-12-03

Dear Nancy,

It was so nice to receive your long letter and to know that everything is fine with you! After working with people for a period of time I certainly consider them friends and it's always great to hear from friends!

Yes, we have been aware of the Oregon law and the general trend of more openness across the country. Nebraska hasn't moved much in that direction although there have been some changes for those born after September 1988. When they become 21 years old, they are entitled to their medical history and their original birth certificate. Of course, the big difference is that birth mothers having a child after September 1988 were (and are) informed of this change and they can sign a non-consent to withhold the birth certificate, if they want. For someone born before that date the birth mother can register a consent or a non-consent with the Bureau of Vital Statistics in Nebraska, but few know of that provision in the law.

Everything was so secretive when you were born that your birth mother undoubtedly assumed that it would stay that way forever. It was almost as if they were promised that their secret would never be revealed. (In fact, the promise was probably made in many cases.) So, it's a huge jump to do as Oregon did with the law being retroactive. I can imagine there was and is some consternation on the part of

nebraska
children's home
SOCIETY

3549 Fontenelle Blvd.
Omaha, NE 68104
(402)451-0787
fax:(402)451-0360
www.nchs.org

The Nebraska Children's Home Society provides safe and loving care to children of all ages.

OFFICES
Fremont • Gothenburg
Grand Island • Kearney
Lincoln • Norfolk
North Platte • Omaha
Scottsbluff

the older birth mothers as a result! However, they generally don't fight such laws because they are the "silent opposition."

Interestingly enough, a similar law wouldn't help you any because you have the information that is on your birth certificate, that is, the name! Many times the name is on the adoption decree and people have always had the right to petition the court for that information. The part that is sad is that birth mothers like yours still feel the guilt and shame when society has long ago moved on. They are so concerned that their neighbors, children, etc., will think badly of them when others often don't care or certainly don't have that kind of extreme reaction! Fortunately, adoption is done differently now and I think it's much healthier for all.

I'm sorry to hear about the loss of your mother. I know what it is like to lose parents and it is not fun. I remember finally feeling relief when I realized that my mother lived on in me (and my siblings). You said that you will carry on because that's the way she raised you and there is comfort in that. How fortunate you were to have that kind of relationship with her!

I'm not sure what to suggest as far as your birth mother is concerned. Neither she nor her husband is listed at her previous address. She is not on the Social Security death index, which is fairly current. So, I really don't know where to find her since she (or they) may have gone into a home or some such thing.

nebraska
children's home
SOCIETY

3549 Fontenelle Blvd.
Omaha, NE 68104
(402)451-0787
fax:(402)451-0360
www.nchs.org

The Nebraska Children's Home Society provides safe and loving care to children of all ages.

OFFICES
Fremont • Gothenburg
Grand Island • Kearney
Lincoln • Norfolk
North Platte • Omaha
Scottsbluff

Also, she was pretty adamant about not being contacted again when last I spoke to her. She wasn't angry but rather sad and it was obviously painful for her. In view of her age, I'm reluctant to take the chance of upsetting her again. It sounds terrible but we could wait until she is deceased and then I could possibly locate her children. Does that sound logical? How strongly did your doctor suggest that we pass this information on? I would like to try again but am hesitant.

Let me know what you think.

Thanks for writing.

Sincerely,

Rebecca Crofoot

Caseworker

February 17, 2003

Ms. Rebecca Crofoot
Caseworker
Nebraska Children's Home Society

Dear Rebecca:

It already has been a busy morning in that my car had to be towed to my mechanic and there is still that matter of house cleaning, but I was anxious to get a reply out to you as quickly as possible. Thank you so much for your response. It was warm, informative, and I do appreciate your thoughts.

I had not remembered that my birth mother had been adamant about not being contacted again. I only recall that she was not angry. It was never my intent to cause her or her family any distress. In light of her feelings and her age, the kindest course of action must be to let this information stay unknown. I would hate to think that I caused any kind of problem for my birth mother or her family, now or after her death, with some medical genetic information that might not even be relevant to them. I should have remembered her statement about "… not wanting to open up the past."

And so, it goes. My husband and I are traveling to Nebraska and Iowa, May 24–June 2, 2003, to visit with aunts, uncles, and cousins. This is our first trip to our collective "homes" ever. While in Omaha, I might give a call to the NCHS to see if you have any time for an in-person "hello and thank you." However, if I don't get to see you, please know how very much I have appreciated what you have done for me over the years. You are a marvel!

With best wishes,
Nancy Kacirek Feldman
Portland, OR

nebraska children's home society

3549 Fontenelle Blvd.
Omaha, NE 68104
(402)451-0787
fax:(402)451-0360
www.nchs.org

The Nebraska Children's Home Society provides safe and loving care to children of all ages.

OFFICES
Fremont • Gothenburg
Grand Island • Kearney
Lincoln • Norfolk
North Platte • Omaha
Scottsbluff

04-09-03

Nancy Feldman
Portland, OR
Dear Nancy,

I apologize for not answering you sooner. Sometimes things get a little busy!

I had not remembered that your birth mother was so adamant either and only realized that when I read my dictation of my contact with her.

nebraska
children's home
SOCIETY

3549 Fontenelle Blvd.
Omaha, NE 68104
(402)451-0787
fax:(402)451-0360
www.nchs.org

The Nebraska Children's Home Society provides safe and loving care to children of all ages.

OFFICES
Fremont • Gothenburg
Grand Island • Kearney
Lincoln • Norfolk
North Platte • Omaha
Scottsbluff

I'm enclosing a copy of her letter explaining her feelings. The tone of the letter was much angrier than our phone conversation. When she called she appeared to have calmed down some and it was a pleasant conversation. I had hopes that she may change her mind.

I'm not sure why I had not previously shared a copy of her letter with you. To see her handwriting (which is unique, to say the least!) and what she said will be of great interest to you!

I checked the Social Security death index again and neither her name nor her husband's appears there. The phone has always been unlisted so I have not been able to see if they still reside in their own home.

I have read everything through carefully and just don't feel very comfortable with contacting her again. She would now be 81 years old. I suppose that there is an outside chance that she might be thinking of some contact and no longer knows where to inquire. However, it seems to me that she would have done it some time ago if she were thinking along those lines.

On the other hand, I could try again. The worst that could happen would be for her to not answer and we would know nothing more! I would do this if you feel that it's worth another try. It's certainly your decision. This is one of those circumstances where she might react differently if you were to show up on her doorstep. But, since she has options, she can

nebraska
children's home
SOCIETY

3549 Fontenelle Blvd.
Omaha, NE 68104
(402)451-0787
fax:(402)451-0360
www.nchs.org

The Nebraska Children's Home Society provides safe and loving care to children of all ages.

OFFICES
Fremont • Gothenburg
Grand Island • Kearney
Lincoln • Norfolk
North Platte • Omaha
Scottsbluff

choose to do nothing. This is hardly fair to you but I always struggle with how far to push.

If you do decide that you would like one more attempt, it would be helpful to me if you would write me a note that I could at least quote to her. My words would not be nearly as important as yours. Here we are again, back to square one!

I'll look forward to hearing from you again. By the way I would love to meet you if you are in Omaha. I work Mondays, Wednesdays, and Fridays, but would arrange to meet you another day, if possible.

Sincerely,
Rebecca Crofoot
Caseworker

[This is the handwritten letter from my birth mother and not seen by me until April 2003. Her handwriting was unique and had a pronounced slant to the left.]

4 January 1995

Rebecca Crofoot
Nebraska Children's Home Society

Your letter was one I hoped and prayed I would never receive. The letterhead and contents of the letter was obvious in its purpose. The intrusion into life after 46 years, especially at this time of year was at the very least unsympathetic, and caused me great distress and concern.

Forty-seven years ago I was soon to leave the service with plans to further my education. Prior to my discharge I was involved with a man whom I discovered was married. The realization of this circumstance was so painful I terminated the relationship. I wished no further contact with him and did not inform him of the pregnancy.

1948 and 1949 were the most difficult years of my life. Few options were open at that time and the view of illegitimacy was harsh for not only the mother but also the child. I felt I could not involve my family or friends.

When it became apparent I could not make the arrangements I confided in my sister and brother-in-law. He immediately made the necessary arrangements for the pre-hospital care and the hospitalization. This occurred approximately two weeks before the delivery. At this time the adoption process was begun.

I was informed about the process and I was assured the records would be sealed. I understood this would protect the rights of the child, the adoptive parents and me. I was also informed I would have no contact or knowledge of the child or adoptive parents. I felt this was a logical solution.

I have no recollection of the labor or delivery as I was given scopolamine or "twilight sleep." When I asked if the baby was healthy, the nurse answered "Yes, she…the baby is healthy." After I left the hospital, my brother-in-law told me the baby girl was healthy and the adoption to a caring couple was in process. That is all I have ever known.

With the arrival of your letter I felt betrayed by a legal system, which devised the rules to protect the child and adoption parents from the birth mother and assuring her of her right to privacy.

To this day, the only ones I have confided in were my sister and brother-in-law. I felt strongly at the time and still do that this was best for the child. I have never wished harm to the child and I hope she will feel the same about me.

There is nothing in my family history that should cause concern. I would like to say this is the only event in my life I have been secretive about to my family and friends.

I feel the space of 46 years with no knowledge of the child is too long for any personal involvement to be beneficial to either of us. I expect my right to privacy promised 46 years ago to be honored.

I am interested by what means you used to contact me. Hopefully it was through impersonal agencies such as Social Security. In retrospect I wish I had used a false identity and address.

I will contact you by phone, but I've written this letter because it is important to me you know the facts. Again I say I do not want my name or address divulged to anyone. My family's love and respect means everything to me.

Sincerely,

Becky's Note: *Somehow the date of birth was overlooked and the birth mother should not have been approached in January. Respect for the birth mother's hidden secret should have been treated with greater sensitivity. Many birth mothers of that time kept their feelings completely private, as society had dictated. The stigma of bearing a child out of wedlock was very* *strong and her reactions to the inquiry were reflective of those feelings.*

The method of locating this birth mother had been discussed during the one conversation on the phone. She was assured that it had been done through public records and the reason for the search was never divulged to anyone.

In Nebraska, adoptive parents had to have the child in their home for six months before they could proceed with legal adoption. As a general practice, the Nebraska Children's Home Society asked for a year's waiting period.

Reading the letter from my birth mother was like getting stung by a bee: it hurt. She sounded so angry, and I had never meant to upset her. When she referred to me as "the child," that hurt too. I hadn't been looking for my "real" mommy, but I had been seeking some small acknowledgment. She seemed to want to put as much distance between us as possible.

I thought about it more and more. I went back and re-read Becky's letter that recounted the phone call that she had with my birth mother. They had the phone call after the letter had been sent (within two weeks). My birth mother wasn't angry then. And then I remembered the conversations I had had with so many (too many) friends about rape and how deplorably the victims were treated by not only the authorities, but their own families. I thought of the shameful manner in which these individuals were treated, and in remembering those conversations, I could forgive my birth mother her anger at a man, at her own body, and at an agency that had betrayed her. So I could write the following letter.

April 14, 2003

Ms. Rebecca Crofoot
Caseworker
Nebraska Children's Home Society
Dear Rebecca:

WOW … Your letter was waiting for me when I returned home from a wonderful time in Chicago. My husband was there on company business and I got to tag along and spend time with my Chicago childhood (1960–1964) friend, Barbara. What a wonderful opportunity. We have maintained a friendship for over 40 years, but get few opportunities for in-person exchanges. And so here waits this envelope with two letters, both remarkable in their own right. Thank you for sending them. (And my handwriting is nothing like my birth mother's! Completely different. Whose does it resemble? My mother's, of course. I am smiling as I type this.)

I had some suspicions that were confirmed by my birth mother's letter (her involvement with a married man, how difficult that time was for her, and her need to have this time safely stored in the past.) I was a little saddened by her tone, and thank you for your reassurance that by the time she phoned you, she had appeared to calm down and that you had a pleasant conversation.

Again, I want to state that it was never my intent to cause her or her family any distress. I believe that you and I are both in agreement that we must NOT attempt any further contact for any reason. In light of her feelings and her age, we must let her past that involves myself remain silent and unknown. Although I don't know her and never will, I feel very protective of her.

Thank you for telling me your schedule. We arrive in Omaha on Saturday, May 24th. Monday is the Memorial Day holiday, and on Wednesday we are planning on leaving for several days in Iowa at my husband's childhood home. So what about sometime after lunch on that Wednesday, May 28th? I just want to drop in for a few minutes to give you an in-person thank you and a hug! I will call beforehand, of course.

I treasure our relationship and again want to thank you for sending both letters. You are a marvel!

With best wishes,

Nancy Kacirek Feldman

[We weren't able to meet and two years passed.]

Greetings of the Christmas 2005 season to all of you:

It is again that exhilarating time of year, and please know that we wish all of you a memorable Christmas and New Year. This will be the first of a very different holiday season for us as my dad, George Kacirek, passed from this life on April 23, 2005. I have decided to forego my Christmas letter and instead share what Michael beautifully wrote and read at my dad's California memorial on June 4, 2005.

"All of you here today have been touched by George in different ways, some as family and some as friends. I have been fortunate to have known George in many different capacities and this is my tribute to let you know how I will always remember him.

"I knew George as a father-in-law; a kind, generous person, who was always willing to help Nancy and me when we were first married. He always had suggestions for us, some good, and some not so good.

"I knew him as a grandfather, devoted to his grandson, Forrest. He always wanted him to succeed. He was so happy when he was awarded his Masters in Fine Arts.

"I knew George as an eternal optimist, who was always greeting each day as if it were his last. With George everything was 'the best' or 'absolutely the finest.'

Mom and Dad's 50th wedding anniversary, January 24, 1993. From left: Michael and Nancy Feldman, Forrest Cole, Lucille and George Kacirek.

"I knew George as a businessman. Even in retirement, his mind was active to the very last day. His favorite phrases 'You are going to have to hit it hard now,' and 'When I was at Mobil ...' will remain in my mind forever.

"I knew George as a man, who was in control of his life's schedule even down to the last minutes. He had lists for everything. He took great joy in watching the *Lawrence Welk Show*, and I will always remember him saying, 'Well, let's see what Leno has to say,' after he had taped the Jay Leno show, so he could be in bed by 8:00 p.m.

"And, lastly, I knew George as a devoted husband, who took his wedding vows seriously and he took care of Lucille 'through sickness and in health.'

"In closing, if you are looking down on us all today, George, I want you to know that Nancy is here in a 'smart sport outfit,' instead of her favorite tie-dye. And I hope especially that it is 'sunny and 80' wherever you and Lucille are today. You are missed."

Go well.

Love, Nancy and Michael

This was our Christmas letter for December 2006.

Dear Friends and Family:

Again, it is that time of year to wish each and every one of you Merry Christmas and Happy New Year.

As you know, it has been a year of firsts for us. A big first was when I did not write my traditional Christmas letter, but used instead Michael's wonderful eulogy for my dad. My father is deeply missed. With his passing, Michael and I were suddenly put into the position of having no parents. We lost our mothers and Michael's dad in such rapid succession, but considered ourselves fortunate to not only have had my dad an additional four years, but to have him living in Portland.

Then in February 2005, Forrest moved to Portland from Las Vegas. The summer of 2005 had been a most difficult one for my dad. Forrest had returned to Spain that summer to work for his friends at their hostel, but I asked him to come to Oregon for a month due to my dad's serious health complications. Frankly, I did not think that he would last that summer, but he delighted us with his persistence.

In that month Forrest recognized his Grandpa's fragile state and made the decision to move to Portland after he completed the fall semester teaching at UNLV. He wasn't certain how long he would stay in Portland, but he wanted to spend time with Grandpa and us, while there was still time. He lived with us and spent time every day with his Grandpa, helping out as Dad was placed in palliative care (weekly nurse visits) to hospice care. Kaiser Health Plan was wonderful in providing all of this care in Dad's own apartment in his assisted living facility, so that he never had to leave familiar surroundings. He was placed in hospice care three weeks before he died.

We were expecting, actually hoping, that he would be around for six months. But he was so worn out, so tired. I know that this may surprise some of you who talked to him in the months, weeks, and even days before his death, because he always sounded so strong on the telephone. But he always had the capability to pull himself up when the phone rang. He never wanted to appear weak. Although he readily, and gladly, used a walker from 2001, he never used it when I would take him to his monthly barbershop visits. His mind was sharp until the end (we paid bills the day before he died), but his body just simply was worn out. Robert, the hospice nurse, recommended that we spend more daytime hours and stay overnight with Dad, even though his residence had aids that checked on him every 30 minutes during the night. So, Michael, Forrest, and I divided up the day, and alternated nights.

On the day before he died, I had spent the whole day with him getting a hospital bed delivered and hiring a nurse to come in for one day a week. At 5:00 p.m., Michael arrived to spell me, and Dad simply said, "Michael, I want you to know how much I deeply appreciate all that you have done for Lucille and myself, but I want Nancy to stay tonight because I am going to die." I was shocked, but I stayed. Michael was there when we put Dad to bed, and it was then when I saw how comfortable he was in the new hospital bed (it had become so difficult for him to get into his own bed) that I knew he was going to pass away.

As the sun briefly peeked out as it came up on that Saturday morning, he slipped quietly from this life and from us. I know that I speak honestly for the three of us in saying we will always miss him, but we never begrudged the fact that he needed to let go. …

I had a rough time of it. I will not deny it. Kaiser Hospice wisely provided grief counseling for me. I attended weekly group meetings for eight months. I valued that experience greatly. I learned so much from all of the sessions, the coordinator, and my fellow grievers. In April I had a complete hysterectomy for a non-cancerous problem. The prognosis is excellent and I have not felt so good in several years.

In June I was asked back to the shop, Front Porch Mercantile, that I had filled in for a friend the summer before. So I became the Monday afternoon shop girl. The shop carries a variety of antique, garden, collectibles, and cutesy stuff. It will close this January, and I will join Michael in the part-time job search. I have enjoyed working there. In fact, I worked there today, and it snowed. And snow is always a great trigger for these letters, don't you know? And so, I have come full circle in this letter to tell you how we all have been, that we think of you, all of you, and remember all of the fun times in the past and we look forward to creating many more memories.

It is our fervent wish that you enjoy the merriest of Christmases and happiest of New Years. Never hesitate to visit us. We would gladly share the Pacific Northwest with you.

Go well.

Love, Nancy and Michael

January 15, 2007

Ms. Rebecca Crofoot
Caseworker
Nebraska Children's Home

Dear Ms. Crofoot:

Hello again. It has been about four years since our last correspondence. I hope that all is well with you and the NCHS. I continue to get my NCHS newsletters and am always inspired about the great work that you do.

You may recall our correspondence of four years ago regarding my genetic discovery that I had Hemochromatosis (iron overload) and whether or not it was a good idea to contact my birth mother about this with respect to possible impact on her children. We made the right decision not to worry about this. I was being monitored with bi-yearly blood tests and when it was noted that my blood ferritin levels began to increase, I started a series of weekly blood lettings (a pint taken at a time) to attempt to bring the level down. A good level is 50 or below, mine were 300+. Organ damaging levels are in the 1000's, so I was in no danger, but it was considered a good idea to bring them down.

Shortly after I started these, I had an episode of extreme abdominal cramping which I thought was a gallbladder attack. My gallbladder was fine, but the ultrasound revealed that there were "shadows" on my pancreas. In addition, it was noted that my liver was covered with cysts. After meeting with the surgeon I decided I would rather not sit and stew about what might possibly be, but take action. I elected to have surgery in September of 2004, where the body and tail of my pancreas and my spleen were removed. The masses turned out to be multi-chambered cysts, and nothing was cancerous.

As the surgeon told me, "You are one of the very few that gets good news from me."

I am delighted with my good fortune. Is any of this connected to iron overload? Maybe, but most likely not. Since extra iron stores stay in the body, especially the heart and liver, it has been recommended that I modify my diet. My pancreas was cut in half and diabetes is a potential possibility. Dietary restrictions such as minimal sweets and alcohol intake can only benefit my whole system. I am sorry for the long drawn-out medical update, but I am just so grateful that all has turned out so well for me. My husband was so pleased with our "best ever possible" prognosis that he took me on a cruise in March 2005. When we returned home, my father had been shifted from palliative to hospice care. My enclosed Christmas letter of this year brings you-up-to-date with my father's death in April 2005.

My father was tall and thin. I'm about 5'3" and weight has always been a concern. As I used to explain, "Unfortunately, we don't draw from the same gene pool." Genetics was the only area that I did feel we weren't "connected." Lucille and George Kacirek were my parents. I never questioned that. I never felt that I was someone else's child being raised by kindly strangers. Without computers, with information that no doubt was hand sorted, the NCHS found the perfect, forever home for Baby Girl Carroll, who became Nancy Elaine Kacirek. Again, I am so thankful.

Again, my husband and I plan to visit Omaha sometime in the spring or early summer. We have been communicating since 1994, and I would certainly love to meet you. Let's try to arrange something, okay?

Sincerely,
Nancy Kacirek Feldman
Portland, Oregon

nebraska children's home SOCIETY

3549 Fontenelle Blvd.
Omaha, NE 68104
(402)451-0787
fax:(402)451-0360
www.nchs.org

The Nebraska Children's Home Society provides safe and loving care to children of all ages.

OFFICES
Fremont • Gothenburg
Grand Island • Kearney
Lincoln • Norfolk
North Platte • Omaha
Scottsbluff

February 12, 2007
Nancy Feldman
Portland, OR
Dear Nancy,

It was so nice to hear from you, even though it took me some time to answer you! I'm glad to hear that your health problems are not as bad they could be. I guess we all have our health issues as we get older, but we hope that they are manageable!

At this point, I plan to be in town the week after Memorial Day and would love to meet

nebraska
children's home
SOCIETY

3549 Fontenelle Blvd.
Omaha, NE 68104
(402)451-0787
fax:(402)451-0360
www.nchs.org

The Nebraska Children's Home Society provides safe and loving care to children of all ages.

OFFICES
Fremont • Gothenburg
Grand Island • Kearney

you. Shall we set a time and then it's more definite? However, if it all depends on things in Iowa, we could just talk when you get in town. Let me know & I'll put it on my calendar.

Thanks for keeping in touch!

Sincerely,

Rebecca Crofoot

Caseworker

February 28, 2007

Dear Rebecca –

Thanks so much for your note. Since I wrote we have switched our Omaha visit from Memorial Day to Easter. Will you be in town? We arrive on Wed, 4/4, and leave Monday, 4/9. Do you have any time available on Thursday, 4/5? I'm staying at my cousin's. Just drop me a note if you're free. I look forward to our first in-person meet!

Nancy Feldman

April, Easter time 2007, and Michael and I were going to the Fontenelle Boulevard Nebraska Children's Home. This was my first visit since my Girl Scout troop went to deliver valentines to the resident kids in the 1950s. I had to keep biting the side of my mouth, and I started to lose it even before we got out of the car. I did not want to be crying so much that no one could understand me.

We came in the front door and saw what I thought was the first waiting room (on the left) that my parents had to wait in when they were applying for a baby. I remembered my mom talking about that room. I could hear her voice and I started crying again. Or had I ever stopped?

Then a young woman led Michael and me into the front room and I totally lost it. I was so grateful that there were *two* boxes of Kleenex! The young woman said, "Many tears are shed in this room." I know this room: this is the room where the magic happens. A child, man, and woman become a family here. I felt like I was in such a spiritual place.

Then in came Becky, just back from knee surgery, and we both felt comfortable with her from the very beginning. We talked and talked and talked: about growing up in Omaha, Czechs, Touhy, Wahoo and Weston, Nebraska, where my dad had grown up, riding horses at Hillside Stables (now a shopping mall), living in the Midwest, being adopted and more. The hours flew by. I kept thinking, "She's going to want to wrap this up. She is going to want us to leave." But we never felt rushed.

Becky asked me where I thought I would go from here. Would I want to seek contact with any possible siblings? I have thought about this a lot. I told Becky about going on the Internet and typing in the name Carroll for various Midwestern states. I told her of the printed lists ("Pages and pages," Michael said.) of CARROLLs who had died in 1931, 1932, and 1933 (about the time my birth mother's father died). I looked at names and names and found nothing. But I thought that if I had my birth mother's full name, my Internet search would be defined and I could gather information without disrupting anyone's life.

Becky said that she would be glad to check the Social Security death index a couple of times a year with some gentle prompting and then she would help me get my original birth certificate. With that I could conduct my search. I thought that this sounded like a good idea.

Michael took a picture of me outside the building. I was smiling through my tears. So we were off to the family to continue the Easter celebration and I was feeling so good!

Me in front of the Nebraska Children's Home Society building.

nebraska
children's home
SOCIETY

3549 Fontenelle Blvd.
Omaha, NE 68104
(402)451-0787
fax:(402)451-0360
www.nchs.org

The Nebraska Children's Home Society provides safe and loving care to children of all ages.

OFFICES
Fremont • Gothenburg
Grand Island • Kearney
Lincoln • Norfolk
North Platte • Omaha
Scottsbluff

April 11, 2007

Dear Nancy,

It was so nice to visit with you and your husband! Thank you for making the effort. I hope you had a wonderful Easter with all of those relatives!

I did check the Social Security Death Index again and nothing appears there. It's good to know you have good genes!

Thanks again.
Sincerely,
Rebecca Crofoot
Caseworker

Becky's Note: *Nebraska law requires either permission from the birth parent(s) or proof of death before Vital Records can release an original birth certificate. In Nancy's case, she knew the last name of her birth mother, but she would need the first name, birth date or other information from the original birth certificate before she could trace her birth mother.*

The agency's record contains background information recorded at the time of Nancy's birth but only non-identifying information can be shared without the release of the original birth certificate. Other states had different versions of similar laws in the 1940s.

April, 18, 2007

Dear Becky:

Thank you so much for taking so much time with both Michael and me. It was such a wonderful experience to meet you after our long paper relationship. I will never forget being in that most special room. One can just feel all the love that was generated from there.

Thank you with all my heart. Here's to a long future relationship!

Nancy

nebraska children's home society

3549 Fontenelle Blvd.
Omaha, NE 68104
(402)451-0787
fax:(402)451-0360
www.nchs.org

The Nebraska Children's Home Society provides safe and loving care to children of all ages.

OFFICES
Fremont • Gothenburg
Grand Island • Kearney
Lincoln • Norfolk
North Platte • Omaha
Scottsbluff

May 20, 2007

Dear Nancy,

Like you, I want to add it was really fun to meet and have the chance to visit. You are right in that we have had a long relationship and can look forward to more contact.

I'll expect to hear from you occasionally and I'll check again. It's a mixed blessing since good genes are to be appreciated, as you mentioned! Take care and thank you for the nice card.

Sincerely,
Rebecca Crofoot
Caseworker

Again, time passed quickly and then it was Christmas 2008.

It is Christmas time and Michael and I want to wish each and every one the merriest of Christmases and happiest of New Years. This year in order to attempt to preserve resources; natural and financial, I will be doing a first by sending some of you my Christmas greetings cyber-style.

As some of you know, Spring and Summer brought ill health to our Forrest. Although we will never be certain, it appears that his troubles began with an arthroscopic knee surgery in April. Almost immediately, he began having trouble with retention of fluid in his legs and then his abdomen. In all, he put on 50 pounds of fluid.

After an extensive series of tests, it was found in October that he had a serious kidney ailment,

It is Christmas time and Michael and I want to wish each and every one the merriest of Christmases and happiest of New Year's. This year in order to attempt to preserve resources, natural and financial, I will be doing a first by sending some of you my Christmas greetings cyber-style.

As some of you know, Spring and Summer brought ill health to our Forrest. Although we will never be certain, it appears that his troubles began with an arthroscopic knee surgery in April. Almost immediately, he began having trouble with retention of fluid in his legs and then his abdomen. In all, he put on 50 pounds of fluid. After an extensive series of tests, it was found in October that he had a serious kidney ailment, cause unknown, and he was started on steroids. The steroids caused suppression of his immune system and after an emergency hospital admission, it was found that he had an infection on his pacemaker. The doctors called the infection a "Super Bug." He was started on super antibiotics and discharged after 2 weeks with an IV in place. He then had to give himself twice daily infusions of antibiotics. He was off of work for the whole month of November. Michael made an early November trip to NY to be with Forrest (thank you again Beth and Tom for your generous miles donation) and then we both went for Thanksgiving week. We are thrilled to tell you that the infection appears to be gone and Forrest has returned to work. The kidney problem still exists and won't be going away without steroid therapy, but Forrest's condition is so much better now than it was this fall. He now has a wonderful team of doctors who are most definitely healers.

Michael and I realized this past year that we both needed jobs. Michael has demonstrated water filtering systems, sold protective coverings for marble, pool fences and National Self Employed Association memberships. He plans to work for a medical insurance company in 2009. He still plays harmonica at bimonthly blues jams. I actually think his singing voice is even better than before. I registered with 3 temp agencies, but found out I had been out of the office too long (6 years) and my computer skills were severely outdated (doesn't anybody do Volkswriter anymore?). In August, Petsmart hired me as a part-time cashier. As far as I am concerned I have the greatest job. I pat silky dog heads all day long (all the dogs know that I have cookies!) and get to listen to excited children tell me all about their pets. Sometimes I wonder what ever took me so long to find this perfect job!

In closing with our best holiday wishes, I want to share the following which has the true meaning of this magical season: The short story, "The Gift of the Magi," by O'Henry, has always been a

istmas
s her hair,
s a watch
es. It never

ery moving
oved first to
to somehow
through
e quilts
e only
it off. Half

...come from my Grandma McCann from a quilt that she had pieced in the 1940's. I finished Grandma's blue blocks with red. The second quilt was assembled by me, made up of materials donated by my water aerobics class friends. I took their picture holding the quilt for the soldier to have faces to put with the quilt. Michael sent both of the quilts from our local UPS Store, where we have an account. Two weeks after the second quilt was sent, Irum, who owns the UPS store, called me and said she had an envelope addressed to me, but with her address. She said, "The return address is American Hero Quilts. Do you make quilts to donate? Because if you do, I believe I have something for you." I went into the shop and was astounded by what waited for me: SIX huge boxes filled with store fabric samples that a friend could no longer keep. SIX HUGE BOXES of pre-cut fabric squares in cashmere wool, wool plaid, wool and COTTON. Packages and packages of cotton. I took them all and got busy locating quilters. I donated fabric to three quilters groups (all church affiliated) and each group had at least one quilter who was making quilts for American Hero Quilts. The Lake Oswego Methodist Church has a member who makes a quilt a week for AHQ. And I kept enough material to make two more quilt tops for AHQ. One mis-addressed envelope created a wonderful giving tree! It was indeed meant to be. When I went back in to thank Irum again and told her of the many groups and returning soldiers that will benefit from her kindness, she wept. And for me, the friendships that have been created are treasures.

May the magic of this season, the warmth that it generates, and the good will that it inspires be yours.

Go well. With love,

Nancy and Michael

Christmas letter.

cause unknown, and he was started on steroids. The steroids caused suppression of his immune system and after an emergency hospital admission, it was found that he had an infection on his pacemaker. The doctors called the infection a "Super Bug." He was started on super antibiotics and discharged after two weeks with an IV in place. He then had to give himself twice daily infusions of antibiotics. He was off of work for the whole month of November. Michael made an early November trip to NY to be with Forrest (thank you again Beth and Tom for your generous miles donation) and then we both went for Thanksgiving week.

We are thrilled to tell you that the infection appears to be gone and Forrest has returned to work. The kidney problem still exists and won't be going away without steroid therapy, but Forrest's condition is so much better than it was this fall. He now has a wonderful team of doctors who are most definitely healers.

Michael and I realized this past year that we both needed jobs. Michael has demonstrated water-filtering systems, sold protective coverings for marble, pool fences and National Self Employed Association memberships. He plans to work for an insurance company in 2009. He still plays harmonica at bimonthly blues jams. I actually think his singing voice is even better than before. I registered with three temp agencies, but found out I had been out of the office for too long (six years) and my computer skills were severely outdated (doesn't anybody do Volkswriter anymore?). In August, PetSmart hired me as a part-time cashier. As far as I am concerned I have the greatest job. I pat silky dog heads all day long (all the dogs know that I have cookies!) and get to listen to excited children tell me all about their pets. Sometimes I wonder whatever took me so long to find this perfect job.

In closing with our best holiday wishes, I want to share the following which has the true meaning of this magical season: The short story, "The Gift of the Magi," by O'Henry, has always been a favorite Christmas story of mine. It is about a young couple with no money to buy Christmas presents for one another. They each sacrifice a personal treasure (the wife cuts and sells her hair, the husband pawns his father's watch) in order to buy a gift for the other. The wife buys a watch fob for her husband and the husband buys beautiful combs for his wife's tresses. It never fails to touch me with its sweetness.

The following is my 2008 version of "The Gift of the Magi": This past spring I heard a very moving story about American Hero Quilts. Sue Nebekar of Vashon Island, Washington, was moved first to tears and then to action about the suicide of a returning Iraq War veteran. She wanted to somehow provide comfort to those physically and emotionally hurt soldiers. She found her way through quilting. She organized a group of friends and they have committed themselves to make quilts until the last soldier is home. They gladly accept quilts from other groups and individuals. The only criteria are that all the quilts be cotton and red, white and blue.

I had such a quilt, started by my Grandma McGann in the 1940s. Grandma had pieced together several blue blocks, to which I added red. The second quilt assembled by me, was made up of materials donated by my water aerobics class friends. I took their picture holding the quilt for the soldier to have faces to put with the quilt. Michael sent both of the quilts from our local UPS Store.

When American Hero Quilts sent me a thank you, they addressed it to me, but sent it to the UPS Store address. Irum, the owner, called to tell me that she had this and to ask about American Hero Quilts. When I told her, she said, "I believe I have something special for you." What Irum had was a treasure of fabric. SIX huge boxes filled with tailor shop fabric samples that a friend could no longer keep. SIX HUGE BOXES of pre-cut fabric squares in cashmere wool, wool plaid, wool and COTTON. Packages and packages of cotton.

I took them all and got busy locating quilters. I donated fabric to three quilters groups (all church affiliated) and each group had at least one quilter who was making quilts for American Hero Quilts. The Lake Oswego Methodist Church has a member who makes a quilt a week for AHQ. And I kept enough material to make two more quilt tops for AHQ. One mistakenly addressed envelope created a wonderful giving tree. It was indeed meant to be. When I went back to thank Irum again and told her of the many groups and returning soldiers that will benefit from her kindness, she wept. And for me, the friendships that have been created are treasures.

May the magic of this season, the warmth that it generates, and the good will that it inspires be yours.

Go well.

With love,

Nancy and Michael

And I handwrote the following note:

Rebecca –

You had a family wedding this past summer, didn't you? I hope it was wonderful.

It's probably time to check the Social Security death records. You said I should remind you about this every so often.

I do appreciate all you've done.

Hoping for a Memorial Day trip. Would love to see you again.

Go well.

Nancy

nebraska children's home SOCIETY

3549 Fontenelle Blvd.
Omaha, NE 68104
(402)451-0787
fax:(402)451-0360
www.nchs.org

The Nebraska Children's Home Society provides safe and loving care to children of all ages.

OFFICES
Fremont • Gothenburg
Grand Island • Kearney
Lincoln • Norfolk
North Platte • Omaha
Scottsbluff

January 30, 2009

Dear Nancy,

It was nice to hear from you! I am glad to know that life goes on as usual with you and your projects! A belated Happy New Year to you.

I checked the SS# Death Index and again your birth mother's name is not on it. I know this news is a mixed blessing for you.

I guess there is not much else to do unless you have some ideas. You can ask me to check again whenever.

Take care and let me know if you want anything else.

Sincerely,
Rebecca Crofoot
Caseworker

P.S. "Forgot to answer! Yes, we had a wonderful wedding—almost as much fun as our wedding! Thanks for asking."

Becky's family at her daughter's wedding.

Becky's Note: *Personal notes and photos exchanged are generally not part of the norm of a caseworker/ client relationship. In this case, however, Nancy and I had known each other and worked together for a long time. An obvious friendship was the result.*

April 12, 2010

Ms. Rebecca Crofoot
Nebraska Children's Home Society
Hello, Rebecca:

And how are you? I've been thinking about Omaha a lot lately. I'm working as a cashier at PetSmart now and my new store manager is from Omaha. She grew up there and even went to Benson High like two of my cousins. It's always a small world.

I don't remember if we told you when we met (three years ago Easter) that my husband is a musician, who plays blues harmonica. His band was invited to participate in a fundraiser for the city of Libby, Montana. So this past August, we traveled there and afterwards went on to Flathead Lake where we stayed with my Uncle John and cousins, Ken and Debbie Kacirek. My Uncle John spent most of his life in Nebraska: Tuohy, then Omaha, Tech High, Creighton for a year and then his lifetime job for Omaha Power. He fell in love in Montana in the 1940s and he and my aunt bought land on the lake in the 1950s. They retired to Montana in the late 1970s.

Sadly, he died last week. He was 90 ½ years old and had a full life until 6 weeks before his death. For that I'm deeply grateful, but for his death I'm very saddened. So, I am reminded by this (and the fact that I didn't get Christmas cards out this year), that it's time to say hello to you, hoping that all is well, and asking that you check the Social Security death records to see if my birth mom is on them.

I plan to travel to Omaha sometime this year. It's looking like summer or early fall. I would very much like to see you again if our schedules permit. I'm planning on going to Creighton as well for I have donated quite the collection of my dad's from when he was in Pharmacy School there. The dean I spoke with, Curt Barr, now owns the Minne Lusa Pharmacy, where I stopped almost every day coming from school. Again, a small world.

I hope that you and yours are well. I loved the picture of your family at your daughter's wedding. What cute people you are, and what a beautiful bride she was!

Go well.
Your friend,
Nancy Feldman
(aka Girl Carroll)

PS: I've been working on a book for over a year. The story came in a dream. The main character is adopted and feels like I did about her parents. Are you surprised?

nebraska children's home society

3549 Fontenelle Blvd.
Omaha, NE 68104
(402)451-0787
fax:(402)451-0360
www.nchs.org

The Nebraska Children's Home Society provides safe and loving care to children of all ages.

OFFICES
Fremont • Gothenburg
Grand Island • Kearney
Lincoln • Norfolk
North Platte • Omaha
Scottsbluff

April 28, 2010

Dear Nancy,

It was fun to receive your chatty letter! You have been busy as usual!

Well, your birth mother passed away in November of 2009. She was 89, which indicates a lot about her genes. I know nothing more than that but could try to establish more.

I am enclosing some forms for you to fill out assuming that you will want to pursue receiving your original birth certificate. You can indicate what you want to do on the Service Plan and return everything to me. Yes, we have loads of forms now!

Call if you want to talk about possibilities. I am in my office all day on Mondays and Fridays and Wednesday mornings.

Good to hear from you. I hate telling you that she is gone but it does open up other avenues. Take care.

Sincerely,
Rebecca Crofoot
Caseworker

Becky's Note: *With proof of Nancy's birth mother's death, she could request her original birth certificate from the State of Nebraska.*

nebraska children's home society

POST ADOPTION SERVICES

The Nebraska Children's Home Society provides services to any person or family who has been associated with adoption either through our agency or elsewhere. We are available to anyone with questions, concerns or specific needs regarding adoption.

The Nebraska Children's Home Society has a rich history of experience and resources which we hope will be of benefit to all clients. The privacy of everyone is respected at all times.

Post Adoption caseworkers will attempt to locate a member of your adoption circle, if requested. The search is conducted through public records and all contacts will be confidential. The caseworker will serve as an intermediary between all parties and all parties have the right to refuse contact.

Predicting how long it will take to process your request is difficult as each case is different. Please be assured that we want to help in any way that we can and as quickly as we can.

NCHS Post Adoption Services.

NEBRASKA LAW RELATED TO RELEASE OF ADOPTION INFORMATION

Nebraska statutes govern the release of identifying information and the Nebraska Children's Home Society staff must adhere to that standard. However, the laws do provide a way to get information and/or to search for biological relatives while protecting the confidentiality of all parties.

Requirements of the law --

- The adopted person must be 25 years of age if they were relinquished before September 1, 1988. Exceptions may be made with written parental permission. 43-137
- The adopted person must be 21 years of age if they were relinquished after September 1, 1988. Exceptions may be made with written parental permission. 43-146.04
- The agency (Nebraska Children's Home Society) must keep the identity of all parties confidential until consents are obtained from all parties. 43-140
- Nebraska law requires the agency to assist as an "intermediary" in a search for biological relatives.. 43-131, 43-140, 43-146.05, 43-146.10, 43-146.14
- An adopted person has the right to file an Access to Birth information form (if of the legal age to search) with Vital Records at the State of Nebraska to see if any consents have been filed on their name. 43-130, 43-131, 43-146.04, 43-146.05
- An adopted person who was relinquished after September 1, 1988 and has reached the age of 21 can file an Access to Birth Information form with Vital Records at the State of Nebraska. They will receive a copy of their medical history which was recorded at the time of their birth. They will also receive a copy of their original birth certificate if there are no non-consent forms filed on their name. 43-146.05
- A birth parent or birth sibling has the right to file a consent form for release of information with Vital Records at the State of Nebraska. 43-127
- A birth parent has the right to refuse contact with the adopted person. 43-132, 43-146.06
- An heir of the adopted person has the right to request information from Vital Records providing that the adopted person is deceased and 100 years has passed since their birth. 43-146.17
- Upon proof of death of the birth parent(s) listed on the original birth certificate, Vital Records will issue the original birth certificate to the adopted person. 43-135

Nebraska law related to release of adoption information.

It's Time to Find Your Family

I received a sympathy card from my friend, Linda Florentine.

"I know that you have resolved that your birth mother did not want any contact, but I know that you could not help but be moved by her passing. God be good to her.
Love you bunches,
Linda"

It felt strange to be sent a sympathy card for someone I didn't know. But Linda was that type of thoughtful friend. She knew that I would feel badly for the loss of someone's sister, wife, mother, or grandmother. It was like feeling sympathy for some celebrity's family. You feel sadness for them, without it affecting your life.

June 4, 2010

Nebraska Bureau of Vital Statistics
RE: Nancy Elaine Kacirek
Hello:

Pursuant to the attached letter from April 22, 1994, I would like to provide you with a current address.

I have resided in Oregon since August 1995, and lived at this address since July 1997. If you have any questions, please do not hesitate to contact me, either by mail or phone.

Thank you.

Sincerely,

Nancy E. Feldman

Portland, Oregon

Oops, forgot to mention something to them!

August 19, 2010

Nebraska Bureau of Vital Statistics

Lincoln, Nebraska

RE: Nancy Elaine Kacirek

Hello:

I sent a letter, dated June 4, 2010, to your office regarding the attached letter, with regards to my current address. I should have also indicated to you that I did this on the advice of Ms. Rebecca Crofoot of the Nebraska Children's Home Society in Omaha. My adoption was arranged by NCHS in 1949. Ms. Crofoot is aware that my birth mother died in November 2009, and she was making arrangements to provide your office with my birth mother's death certificate. When you are in receipt of this document, would you please send a copy of my original birth certificate to the following address.

I was born on January 26, 1949, at the Methodist Hospital in Omaha.

My adoptive parents were George and Lucille (McGann) Kacirek, sadly both deceased.

Thank you.

Sincerely,

Nancy E. Feldman

Portland, Oregon

My hands were shaking when I got the envelope. The letterhead was from the Nebraska Department of Health and Human Services, and it was dated September 24, 2010.

It read:

> Dear Ms. Feldman:
>
> Reference is made to the Request for Access to Birth Information form that you filed with our office on 6-21-94.
>
> We have received a death certificate for the biological mother listed on your original birth certificate. There is a father listed on your original birth certificate so we will need proof of death for him or his signed consent.
>
> Sincerely,
> Staff Assistant I
> Vital Records Office

There were two attachments that were State of Nebraska Instructions to Searchers, and a Dear Sir or Madam letter regarding original birth certificate request.

A FATHER? What do you mean, a father is listed?

So I called and they, of course, couldn't tell me anything. And it wasn't their fault, but still I was upset. I was so frustrated. After all this time! Why is there a father listed? She must have made up some name! Why would she have done that?

So I called Becky the next day with the news. She seemed disappointed too.

Becky: "Oh, wait, a minute. In going through your file, I note too that a father's name was mentioned. Now we did not get this from your birth mother, this came from the hospital of your birth."

Nancy: "The Methodist?"

"Yes, but the name was spelled differently in two places."

"I think she made up a name. Maybe someone told her that was a sure way for the records to be sealed."

"I don't think so. No one at that time would have known that. But maybe somebody suggested it to her at the hospital."

"Maybe it was my mom's friend, Byrle."

"Oh, that's right, your mom did have a friend working there. Maybe she did. Is she still alive to ask?"

"No. That's disappointing, I mean it's not that disappointing, but I guess it is. Well, it looks like we have come to the end. But I have no regrets. It's just a little sad."

"You know, Nancy, I think it's time that you found your family."

I think I haven't heard her correctly. "Really? You really think so?"

"I think you will find that most individuals are very accepting of what some might consider indiscretions on the part of their mother."

"Really?"

"Yes, why don't you think about it for a while and get back to me?"

November 16, 2010

Ms. Rebecca Crofoot
Caseworker
Nebraska Children's Home Society

Dear Becky:

Well, I have thought about "reaching out" to my half-siblings, and I have thought about it, and then thought about it some more. I have never been afraid of making new friends or getting to know people better. My only hesitation in doing this has been my desire not to upset anyone with the announcement of my existence. I have decided to take a risk and reach out, with your help of course. I have completed the paperwork and, voila! Away we go again. It's been about sixteen years since you located my birth mother (just about this time of year too), so that seems like a good sign to start another search.

I know that you are always busy and I want you to know how I appreciate your ever-constant cheerfulness and willingness to go the distance with me. I know that this has been a tough time for you with the death of your brother and I hope that all is going as well as it can. I'll keep you and yours in my good thoughts and prayers.

Here's wishing you a fabulous holiday season. We are leaving next Monday for Thanksgiving in New York with our son, Forrest. It is a great deal different than Portland or Omaha, but the excitement is always the same as we get to be with Forrest. And the Saks Fifth Avenue music and light display is indeed fabulous and reminds me of the great windows at Brandeis [an Omaha department store that has since closed].

Go well.

Your friend,
Nancy Feldman
Portland, OR

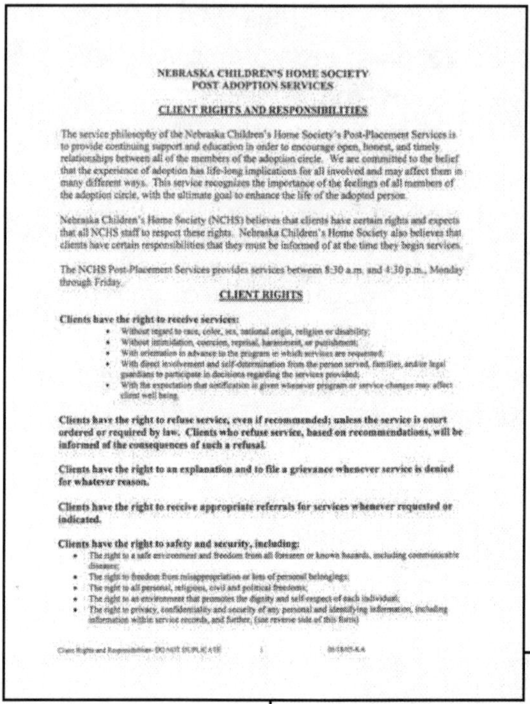

NEBRASKA CHILDREN'S HOME SOCIETY
POST ADOPTION SERVICES

CLIENT RIGHTS AND RESPONSIBILITIES

The service philosophy of the Nebraska Children's Home Society's Post-Placement Services is to provide continuing support and education in order to encourage open, honest, and timely relationships between all of the members of the adoption circle. We are committed to the belief that the experience of adoption has life-long implications for all involved and may affect them in many different ways. This service recognizes the importance of the feelings of all members of the adoption circle, with the ultimate goal to enhance the life of the adopted person.

Nebraska Children's Home Society (NCHS) believes that clients have certain rights and expects that all NCHS staff to respect these rights. Nebraska Children's Home Society also believes that clients have certain responsibilities that they must be informed of at the time they begin services.

The NCHS Post-Placement Services provides services between 8:30 a.m. and 4:30 p.m., Monday through Friday.

CLIENT RIGHTS

Clients have the right to receive services:

- Without regard to race, color, sex, national origin, religion or disability;
- Without intimidation, coercion, reprisal, harassment, or punishment;
- With orientation in advance to the program in which services are requested;
- With direct involvement and self-determination from the person served, families, and/or legal guardians to participate in decisions regarding the services provided;
- With the expectation that notification is given whenever program or service changes may affect client well being.

Clients have the right to refuse service, even if recommended; unless the service is court ordered or required by law. Clients who refuse service, based on recommendations, will be informed of the consequences of such a refusal.

Clients have the right to an explanation and to file a grievance whenever service is denied for whatever reason.

Clients have the right to receive appropriate referrals for services whenever requested or indicated.

Clients have the right to safety and security, including:

- The right to a safe environment and freedom from all foreseen or known hazards, including communicable diseases;
- The right to freedom from misappropriation or loss of personal belongings;
- The right to all personal, religious, civil and political freedoms;
- The right to an environment that promotes the dignity and self-respect of each individual;
- The right to privacy, confidentiality and security of any personal and identifying information, including information within service records, and further, (see reverse side of this form)

Client Rights and Responsibilities- DO NOT DUPLICATE 1 05/18/05-KA

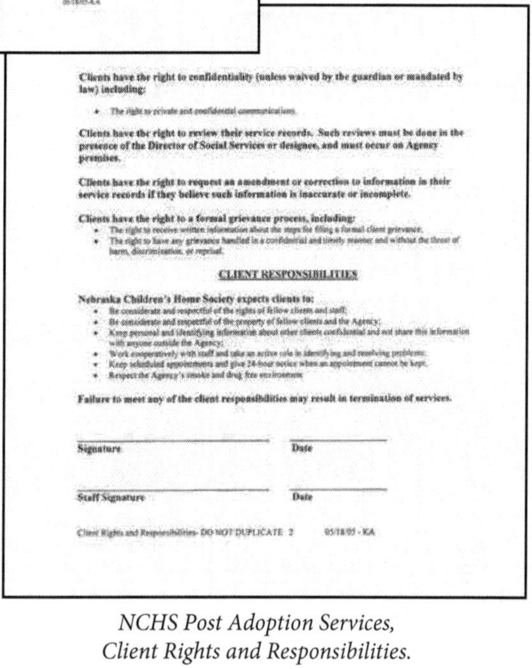

Clients have the right to confidentiality (unless waived by the guardian or mandated by law) including:

- The right to private and confidential communications.

Clients have the right to review their service records. Such reviews must be done in the presence of the Director of Social Services or designee, and must occur on Agency premises.

Clients have the right to request an amendment or correction to information in their service records if they believe such information is inaccurate or incomplete.

Clients have the right to a formal grievance process, including:

- The right to receive written information about the steps for filing a formal client grievance.
- The right to have any grievance handled in a confidential and timely manner and without the threat of harm, discrimination, or reprisal.

CLIENT RESPONSIBILITIES

Nebraska Children's Home Society expects clients to:

- Be considerate and respectful of the rights of fellow clients and staff;
- Be considerate and respectful of the property of fellow clients and the Agency;
- Keep personal and identifying information about other clients confidential and not share this information with anyone outside the Agency;
- Work cooperatively with staff and take an active role in identifying and resolving problems;
- Keep scheduled appointments and give 24-hour notice when an appointment cannot be kept.
- Respect the Agency's smoke and drug free environment.

Failure to meet any of the client responsibilities may result in termination of services.

______________________ ____________
Signature **Date**

______________________ ____________
Staff Signature **Date**

Client Rights and Responsibilities- DO NOT DUPLICATE 2 05/18/05 - KA

NCHS Post Adoption Services,
Client Rights and Responsibilities.

SERVICE PLAN
FOR
POST ADOPTION SERVICES

The Nebraska Children's Home Society recognizes the life-long needs of everyone who has been involved with adoption. The following services are provided through Post Adoption Services at the Nebraska Children's Home Society. Please check which service you are requesting at this time. You may check more than one service, if applicable.

ADOPTED PERSON

______ I am requesting all medical history from the record.

______ I am requesting non-identifying information from the record.

______ I would like a search conducted for my birth mother for the purpose of possible contact.

______ I would like support to establish tribal membership.

____ I am the son/daughter of the adopted person who is now deceased. I would like to search for and have contact with any available members of my parent's birth family.

______ Other: ______________________________________

BIRTH PARENT

______ I would like to update current family medical information for the record.

______ I would like an update on how my birth son/daughter has been doing since my last contact.

______ I would like to search for my birth son/daughter with the possibility of contact with him/her.

______ Other: ______________________________________

SIBLING

______ I would like to search for and have contact with my birth sibling(s).

______ Other: ______________________________________

I realize that this Service Plan may need to be re-evaluated and possibly changed in the future.

Client's Signature *Nancy E. Feldman* Date *11/16/2010*

Caseworker's Signature *Rebecca Crofoot, BA* Date *12/03/2010*

Service Plan for Post Adoption Services.

nebraska
children's home
SOCIETY

3549 Fontenelle Blvd.
Omaha, NE 68104
(402)451-0787
fax:(402)451-0360
www.nchs.org

The Nebraska Children's Home Society provides safe and loving care to children of all ages.

OFFICES
Fremont • Gothenburg
Grand Island • Kearney
Lincoln • Norfolk
North Platte • Omaha
Scottsbluff

COA
Council on Accreditation

December 3, 2010

Dear Nancy,

It was good to hear from you! We received the forms. Thanks. I am returning a copy of the Service Plan for you to keep. I am sending another form that got left out for you to return after having signed the back page. Also, some things for you to read are included. I hope you find them interesting!

I really think that this is a good thing for you to do. Even knowing the cause of death is important and there will probably be so many more things you will discover. Very few people are terribly upset about learning more of their mother's past, in my experience. We will think positive, at least at this point!

I will get started as soon as I can. Our policy is not to approach people during the Holidays though so no results will be seen until January. We find that people are too busy and even too emotional to deal with something new at this time of year. I can do the legwork though and be ready to contact someone then.

I will try to keep you posted. Have a blessed Christmas!

Sincerely,
Rebecca Crofoot
Caseworker

Becky's Note: *A quick search in public records had revealed the name and address of one of the birth mother's children. A letter was sent that asked the recipient to call the agency without revealing the reason.*

> *There are several search engines that can be purchased to aid in searches, but public records of births, marriages, and other information are available many places. That kind of information was necessary in this case because of not knowing the names of the birth mother's children.*

After Christmas 2010, I helped a friend catch some cats that had been abandoned in one of her rental properties. They weren't wild, just a little scared, and then we took them in for a veterinary exam. They had to have this before they could be placed in a no-kill shelter. My generous friend was taking care of these two as if they were her very own. My friend, also an adoptee, had a successful search for her siblings. She was now enjoying *not* being an only child very much.

At my "thank you for your help" lunch, we caught up on each other's news. My son had experienced heartbreak right before Christmas and we talked of how sad that a relationship of five years ended so abruptly, but we were positive that it must have been a "meant to be" situation.

I then told her that I had decided to search for my half-siblings. She nearly came out of her chair with excitement! She pressed me to give her all the information I had, little as it was. She had purchased a new computer program that was the best at gathering information regarding family members. She had done her own search on the Internet and had been faced with several dead ends. And then a search angel had seen her postings and had taken it upon herself to make the connection for her. Being called a search angel was certainly not an exaggeration. She had actually been searching for her birth mother, but came too late as not only had her mother already died, but her two older siblings had died as well. But there were two younger siblings left, and they were now enjoying getting to know one another.

The days ticked by in early 2011. Two phone calls with Becky. No news yet. After the first letter received no response, Becky said that she would send another letter. "Not to worry," she said. "Often, mail doesn't get delivered the first time. Or it gets thrown away."

I told her about my searches on the Internet and that I had come up with some names. She said that was a good thing to do. She added, "If you come up with something that seems plausible, call me and we can talk about it." I thought that was cool, but I didn't have anything that seemed to fit at that point.

> ***Becky's Note:*** *Receiving an unexpected letter from a stranger representing an agency is an easy thing to ignore. Many people think it is a scam and others think it is a mistake. In the second letter, reference was made to information about the recipient's mother but the receiver easily could think it had something to do with a contribution made to the agency. Frequently, a second letter, even a third, is necessary to get a response.*

We had gotten home late from a trip, and I had to wait until Michael finished going through all of his e-mails. I was starting to sort trip laundry and basking in the attention the cats were giving me as the returning hero. He had called out, "I'm done, but I think there's an e-mail that you are going to want to read. It's about your search."

I sat there, reading, completely flabbergasted. How did she get all of this information from the little stuff that I had? What kind of computer program is this? As I read, I did experience shivers of excitement.

From: Deby, (A friend)
Subject: Glimmer of Info
Date: March 7, 2011 1:37:29 PM PST
To: Nancy Feldman

Hi Nancy and Michael,

I found some interesting information from an obit in an Olympia paper, dated 12/13/09:

- Louisa Claire Brown, born January 1920 in Worthington, MN, died 11/2009.
- Graduated St. Paul, Minnesota high school 6/1939. Graduated St. Mary's Nursing School in Rochester, Minn 1943.
- Entered military 8/1943, retired 5/1948, from the Army Nurse Corp.
- Married Roger Dale Brown 3/50 (born 3/1921 in New Orleans, LA) 28 years in the Air Force, was a member of a bombing squad with many missions. He has 2 death dates 10/28/2000 and 10/29/2000.

Think there were 2 daughters and 2 sons born: Catherine, Randell, John, and Claire. Both Catherine and John are deceased. John appears to have died during Desert Storm because it lists military honors, and Cathy is deceased but appears to have graduated a HS in Olympia in 1969.

Were members of a Catholic Church, Olympia.

I can't connect to a CARROLL maiden name but the facts are quite interesting. Not all obits I have been reading indicate a maiden name or list parents' names.

There's a picture accompanying the obit. It's small, but it's there. Let me know what happens!

I looked up the obit; I saw the picture. Is this her? It all sounds right. I called my friend, Carol Taipale, in Los Angeles, knowing that she would still be up. She had always been so interested and supportive in my finding birth family members. In fact, she had probably been more interested many times than I had. I used to tease her that if I found any family, I would send her to the reunions. She had thought it right that I reached out to my birth mother to offer her closure regarding giving me up in that I had had such a charmed life.

I started reading the e-mail to her as soon as she said hello. I was talking so fast, she had to stop me several times. "Slow down, slow down. You're going to hyperventilate!"

"But I'm so excited and I don't even know if I should be! Do you think that she looks like me?" I went on, "The picture is so small."

And Carol said, "Where did you get this information again?" She immediately got on her computer, looked up the obit, and said, "It's going to take me a while to look up some other facts. Are you going to bed now? Are you going to be able to sleep? If I find anything, I will call you. Okay?"

I did manage to go to sleep. I still don't know how I did it. A phone call came at 1:30 a.m., and I just knew it was Carol. She was breathless. "I found her on Minnesota's census for 1925, 1935, and 1945! I'm sorry I woke you; I just couldn't wait! Now I'm excited! When are you calling Becky?"

I got up the next morning and called Becky. She was not in that day, so I left a message on her answering machine: "Will you please call me? I have a name I want to run by you? Thanks, Becky." I hoped that I didn't sound pathetic, but know that I probably did … and desperate. I waited and waited. I knew that Becky often didn't work every day, but waiting was so hard. Carol and I talked several times during that day, and Michael said many times, "Are you ever going to be off of the phone?"

I got the stomach flu that night. So I got up and watched old movies on TV and tried not to think how badly I felt or how much I wanted that phone to ring.

The phone rang at 9:00 a.m.

"Sorry if my voice sounds weird. I've been up all night with stomach flu," I said.

"Oh, I'm sorry. Let me call you back," Becky offered.

"No, no. I need to talk to you now. I need to run a name by you. Was my birth mother's name Louisa Claire Brown?"

Deep breath. Sound of pages being turned. "That's her name."

"Oh, my word. All this time she was just north of me, hiding in plain sight married to a Brown!"

She laughed. "You are right. Now, you know you don't have to wait for a response from my letters. You can write your own. Do you think you'll need any help with that?"

"No, from the obituary I can see two of the sibs' names, and I am going to look them up on WhitePages.Com. I know I am sick but I can hardly breathe from excitement!"

> ***Becky's Note:*** *Nancy had all of the information necessary to make the correct conclusion that she had located the identity of her birth mother. Although there were some restrictions as to what I could reveal, it made no sense to not confirm what she already knew.*
>
> *Helping people like Nancy on her incredible journey is indeed a privilege. At this point, my professional role gradually changed to providing support and encouragement only. We communicated frequently and our relationship continued to develop as a lasting friendship.*

Hello There

It didn't take long to write the letter to my siblings. The words just started flowing. I believe that was because I had been writing it in my head for several weeks. I was swimming a lot of laps then and would compose as I swam. I did not want to come on too strong or demanding, and I did not want to sound as if I was insulting their mother. I so wanted this to be right.

I picked a picture of Mom, Dad, and me in Omaha, hoping that they would see how their mom's indiscretion had a positive end in that it made a family for complete strangers. I kept thinking in my head, *Nothing ventured, nothing gained*, and I began to write.

Mom, Dad, and me, Omaha, 1949.

March 24, 2011

Mr. Randell Brown
Ms. Claire Brown
Dear Randell and Claire:

I want to say at the very beginning that the mood of this letter is not one of sadness; it's joy. Please see the copy of the enclosed picture. The happy family of three. The couple were high school sweethearts, who married after the man had completed Pharmacy School at Creighton University in Omaha, Nebraska. They married at age 25 and tried for several years to add to their joy with the birth of a child. I assume that they went through all the tests available for the time, but had no luck with conception. So they applied to the Nebraska Children's Home Society for a baby girl. They waited for a year, and then in March 1949, the call came that said, "Mrs. Kacirek, congratulations, you're a mother." I was an adored only child and my earliest memories are that I was loved and that I was adopted.

I was born on January 26, 1949, at the Methodist Hospital in Omaha, Nebraska. My birth mother was Louisa Claire Carroll, your mother. Your mother provided a wonderful gift to two strangers in search of a family. It is most likely that your mother never saw me, and certainly did not get to hold me. I do know that through the slip of an attending nurse when she asked if the baby was okay, the nurse said, "Yes, she's … the baby is fine." In her own words, your mother said, "1948 and 1949 were the most difficult years of her life." I can only guess how she suffered. She was dating another officer, who failed to tell her that he was married. How betrayed she must have felt, and then to discover that she was pregnant. She had a sister and brother-in-law, who lived somewhere near Omaha and they were her only confidants. They put her in contact with the Nebraska Children's Home, and took care of her after I was born. No one else ever knew what had happened.

In 1994, after a doctor's insistence that I should seek out my family medical history, I discovered that my birth mother had not died after my birth, which is what I had always believed. I also discovered that a great deal of information was available to me from my chart at the Nebraska Children's Home. I can honestly say that the discovery of this new information was overwhelming. No more questions as to where this curly hair came from! I found that I yearned to know more, and so I was assigned to a caseworker named Rebecca Crofoot. We began a relationship of lengthy correspondence and phone calls where we discussed my adoption and what it meant to me. Becky has been a wonderful guide and inspiration throughout the past 17 years.

I wanted to thank my birth mother for all that she had to endure with "our" pregnancy and let her know that I had been raised by loving parents. Becky accomplished this and had a long phone conversation with your mother in January 1995. She did not feel that contact after so long of a time would work, but she was pleased to hear that all was well with me. I only got to know that she was married and had children and grandchildren living near her. I too was pleased that she had experienced a fulfilling life. Becky asked your mom if she'd like to send me any message and her reply (which still brings tears to my eyes) was: "Tell her that I always loved her."

I know that you lost your mother in November 2009. From the obituary and memory book I read how beloved she was, and I learned the sad news that you had lost your dad and siblings Cathy and Jack before. I am a complete stranger, but please know that you have my deep sympathy for all of these losses. My mom died in March 2001, and my dad April 2005. These are not things that we recover from, but we live on with joy because these special and wonderful people existed and shaped our lives.

I moved to Portland, Oregon, in 1995, from Los Angeles, where I had lived since 1964. Three years ago, I started working at a holiday show in Olympia. Often my husband, Michael, and I have gone to Seattle for concerts or exhibits. Whether we drive or take the train, we always pass through Olympia. You can't imagine my surprise that you were living just north of me. All this time, we were so close. It might seem like a lot to ask, but I would like to meet the two of you. I am not expecting anything, other than some information. I would like to see any pictures you might have.

I always wondered what my birth mother and her family looked like. I was raised an only child and I never missed an opportunity to make new friends, always being the sort of person who thought "the more, the merrier." But I realize I have just thrown a tremendous amount of new information at you. I have put a lot of thought into making this contact. There is a risk that there might be rejection as my intrusion in your lives might be unwelcome. But I decided that I would rather venture the risk than not. I wrote you together so you could both have all of this in front of you. Please consider it, but whatever your decision, I will gladly accept it. Please know, as far as I am concerned, there is no right or wrong answer.

If you wanted to verify any of this, you could contact Rebecca Crofoot at the NCHS in Omaha for confirmation.

Thank you.

Nancy Elaine Feldman

Portland, Oregon

Days are going by very slowly. V E R Y S L O W L Y. Beginning to worry.

And then came April 12, 2011. I come home from swimming to find Michael smiling.

"What happened?"

Bigger smile. "She called. Sit down. I talked to her. Read the note I took."

The note read: "Received your letter and would like to talk with you. Sounded pleased to have gotten the letter. Call her at work or home."

"How did she sound? Was she happy or upset? Does she really want me to call her at work?"

"She sounded excited. She did not sound angry or upset. I really think she wants you to call her now, not tonight. "

OH MY GOD! Somebody called!

I walked around the house for several minutes. I truly did not know what to do next. Michael followed me to the computer room and said, "Here, sit down, compose yourself, I'll get you some tea. Go ahead and call her at work. I told you that she sounded like she couldn't wait until tonight."

Claire answered on the first ring, and said, "Nancy?" Although she asked me what I would consider qualifying questions, she was friendly from the beginning. She wanted to know what I knew about my birth mother, and so I read the information that NCHS had given me in 1994, to her. When I told her about the sister and brother-in-law, who had lived near Omaha, Nebraska, and helped my birth mother, she exclaimed that she knew whom that was referring to. I also read her the letter that my birth mother had written to Becky after the initial contact in 1994.

She kept saying, "Poor mom. Poor you."

We talked for one hour that afternoon and then two hours that night. She had me read a lot of Becky's and my correspondence that night. She continued to marvel that neither Becky nor I had ever given up. And she was so complimentary that I had accepted "Mom's" refusal for contact. She had checked with several cousins during the day, and everything I had said coincided with the information I had. She talked about everyone in her family and gave me birth dates and birth places and experiences.

She told me several times, "I have been missing Mom so much lately. I have been wanting to talk about her, go over all of the Mom stories and everyone I know has heard them so much, and now, as if an answer to my prayers, comes you, and you want to hear everything. We may have lost you for a lot of years, but I'm never going to let you go ever again. I feel like I can say that I love you already!"

I cried a lot. Claire misses her mom a lot. I am sorry for that. I know full well how tough that can be.

We promised we were going to send emails.

> From: Claire
> Sent: Tuesday, April 12th, evening
> To: Nancy
>
> This picture would have been taken just about a month before we lost her so it's not the best picture but I wanted you to have something now. I'm on the left with the dark hair but some gray showing. Yes, that's right, I'm the youngest, but the only with gray hair! What about you—do you have gray hair?

I sure hope this gets through. I so wanted you to see a good picture of her.

Also, here is mom's story that she shared with her hospice volunteer. We just loved it. And we learned things that we had never known.

The Story of Louisa Claire Brown.

My name is Louisa Claire Brown. My maiden name was Carroll. I was born in January of 1920, in Worthington, Minnesota. I had three sisters and two brothers, who were twins. My two older sisters were Helen and Margaret. The oldest had red hair and she was feisty. Margaret, the next eldest, had black hair and her nickname was Maggie. The oldest sisters were bossy and fought a lot. The twin boys, Elmer and John were next. They were both sweet and funny, but full of mischief. I was the fourth and Dolly was the last and two years younger than me.

My dad's name was Elmer John Carroll. My mother's name was Virginia Louisa O'Rourke. They met in Wisconsin. My mother was a school principal and my dad was a teacher. After they married, my mother had to quit working, as married women were not allowed to teach or work at a school. I always thought this was so unfair. They moved to Worthington then and I don't remember what kind of work Dad did then.

My mother was beautiful and had thick blue-black hair that she wore in a bun. She was always very frail. Her mother, Grandma O'Rourke, lived with us and always told us not to sit on our mother's lap or hug her too hard. Grandma O, as we called her, did all the household work. She was bossy and even my dad did what she told him to do.

My mother died when I was six from a hemorrhage. All of the children were sent to live with relatives. Helen, the eldest, went to live with one aunt and uncle in a small town in Wisconsin. Dolly, the baby, went to Detroit to live with Uncle Herman and Aunt Marie. Aunt Marie was from France, and spoke both French and English. She taught French to Dolly. They doted on her and bought her beautiful clothes. Maggie, the twins, Elmer and John, and I went to an aunt and uncle's farm in Wisconsin. We were near to where Helen was and we got to see her sometimes. Our aunt and uncle were good people, but were overwhelmed with four extra children. They had four children of their own. They had a son, and he was mean to the twin boys, but always behind his parents' backs. We were there about six months, and then Maggie wrote to our dad and told him we were all going to run away. Right away he sent money for train fare for us to go to St. Paul as he had moved there after mother died.

Dad knew the governor of Minnesota as they had taught school together. The governor served two terms and then went to be a US Senator. Our dad had an important job with the state, but I can't remember what it was now.

Dad was living in an apartment in St. Paul. After we returned, Dad sent for our oldest sister, Helen. She was happy where she was, but finally agreed to come home. Aunt Marie and Uncle Herman in Chicago wanted to keep the baby, Dolly. They had no children of their own, but Dad wanted us to be together. Grandma O came to St. Paul to care for us and run the household. I was so glad to have my Dolly back home that I took her to school for Doll Day and told everyone that she was my doll.

In the next apartment the two MacGregor sisters lived. One was Henrietta and the other Lenore. Dad and Henrietta eloped to Bemidji and our Grandpa Carroll, Dad's dad, drove all the kids up there a few days later. We didn't think anything was out of the ordinary that we went on their honeymoon with them.

We called Henrietta "Honey" or "Mom." She was a professional woman who had beautiful furniture, china, sterling silver, and best of all, a record player.

It was hard on my oldest sister, Helen, when Dad remarried. She had the most memories of our mother.

We all moved into what we always called "The Little White House." It was not too big, but held us all. It had a back porch where the twins slept. Grandma O then moved back to Wisconsin to live with her daughter. We then moved to the Bloom House for a short time, and then to the "Big House," which was a big two-story house with a basement and attic. Dad rented the house and they rented out some rooms to boarders—women who worked at the capitol building.

"Honey" worked at the capitol also. Dolly and I were allowed to visit them if we asked permission. We went once and I told a man that Dolly could say the Lord's Prayer in French and he didn't believe me. I told Dolly to prove it. She knelt on the marble steps, made the sign of the cross and said the prayer in French. I was so proud of her. Dolly and I were not only sisters, but also best friends. We never needed anyone else to play with.

In summer, the older kids went to Worthington to visit their friends for two weeks. Dolly and I went to stay with Honey's parents, Grandma and Grandpa MacGregor. They treated us just like all their other grandkids. We went with Grandma to a quilting bee and sat under the frame and watched the ladies' feet. They took us to the Lutheran Church where the service was all in Norwegian. They told our parents we were so good even though we couldn't understand a word. We were supposed to sleep upstairs, but there was no electricity. It was dark and we were scared and came downstairs. Grandma and Grandpa said it was o.k. and we could sleep on Grandpa's daybed downstairs.

We were staying with them when we found out our dad's dad, Grandpa Carroll, had died. They were so nice to us. Dolly and I were so sad. It had been so unexpected and our parents were busy with funeral arrangements, so we stayed for several extra days. Grandpa and Grandma let us have cinnamon toast and tea with honey in bed for three days.

Grandma tucked us in every night and read several stories to us. We knew that we were too old for that special treatment, but we just ate it all up.

When I was about 10, Dad got sick and Honey took him to the Mayo Clinic in Rochester, Minnesota. Dad had colon cancer and had a colostomy. He came home and never went to work in the capitol again, but people brought his work to the house for him to continue working.

Dad died when I was 12 years old. Family members and others told Honey that we were not her kids and she didn't need to take care of us. She said, "Oh, yes, they are my children," and kept us together.

We stayed in the same house and Honey continued to rent out rooms because there was no Social Security and no life insurance.

I remember that the summers in Minnesota were brutal. One summer it got to be 112 degrees. Honey told Dolly and I to close the windows and drapes when we got up and turn on the fans. Honey had fixed up a room in the basement where we had our toys. She had given us beautiful doll furniture. Dolly and I said, "Let's play life." It's what we called our play when we would use our imaginations the most. One day we decided to go to the North Pole. We went to the attic and put on heavy coats in the heat of summer. Honey came home for lunch and was horrified when she found us up there. She made us take off the coats, go downstairs, and she put ice on our necks.

Sister Helen married her high school sweetheart and stayed in Minnesota. Maggie went to nurses' training in Chicago. Both of the twins joined the military and made that their careers.

After high school I wanted to go to nurses' training. I could have gone to a local hospital, but Honey wanted me to go to St. Mary's in Rochester, because they were the hospital where the Mayo Clinic sent their patients. Honey said Dad had had wonderful care there and she wanted the best training for me even though she had to pay for it. I was there for three years. The nuns were strict, but wonderful teachers. Only about half of my class made it to graduation. I made it, and passed the boards. Then Dolly came to St. Mary's two years after I got there and also graduated. I always thought that Dolly was smarter than I, but I loved nursing so much, I think I was a better nurse. Whenever I looked for work, I got the job right away when I told them I had graduated from St. Mary's.

Dolly later married a doctor and had lots of children. Both she and her husband died too young.

I joined the Army Air Corps in August 1943, and was discharged in May 1948, as a 1st Lieutenant. I had wanted to become a flight nurse, but I was too short. It was a big disappointment to me.

About the time I left the Army, Honey became ill. Maggie and I went back to St. Paul and took care of her until she died. Honey was so important to me and I was happy to care for her and try to repay all her love and kindness.

While I was deciding where I wanted to settle down, Maggie invited me to spend Christmas of 1949 with her and her family in El Paso, Texas. Her husband was in the Air Force and his best friend was Clarence

Henry Brown. An older brother had always called him "Buster," and lots of family and friends called him "Bus." He was tall and handsome and we fell in love. We eloped in December, but didn't tell anyone. We were church married in March 1950.

We had four children. Two boys and two girls. Catherine Lenore, John Henry, Randall Clarence, whom we called "Dutch" and Claire.

My husband was career Air Force. We traveled to many places and I had hoped he would get stationed in Germany, and how wonderful that was when it actually happened. We went to Frankfort, and were fortunate to get to be there for four years, because Bus requested a longer assignment. We were so happy when that was approved. It turned out to be a wonderful place to live.

We settled in Olympia when Bus retired and always loved it here.

Our eldest Cathy got married young, right out of high school. She married her high school sweetheart. One year later, she was in a car accident and died. She lingered for several days. That was horrible to watch. I can truthfully say that I have never recovered from that. A parent is not supposed to bury their child.

Next came John, who decided that he too would be career military. He served twenty years, but retained active reserve status. Sadly, he died during Desert Storm.

Next is Dutch. He married Laura, and they have two wonderful boys, Jack and Jason. Each boy married wonderful women and they have children who are the lights of my life.

My darling husband got sick in 2000. He was having a lot of different problems and his body just shut down. It's so hard for a nurse to watch a relative in failing health. You feel so helpless. And yet we had a special year in 2000: we celebrated 50 years of marriage and both of our grandsons got married. Then the end of December came and my darling Bus passed from this world. I miss him every day.

My baby, Claire, has no children, but her pets have always been her kids and we treated them like grandchildren. When I hung up pictures in my house of the kids and the grandkids, I always included Claire's animals.

After Bus died, I sold our house and moved to this apartment. I have enjoyed it here. I'm close to church, hairdresser, restaurants I like, and it's not too far from my kids.

I am so grateful to have my two children so close by. They are wonderful to me.

And there it was—her story. I was absolutely astounded. The framework that I had was now filled in. Of course, there was nothing about me, but that didn't matter. What an incredible story! How wonderful of Claire to be willing to share this with me. *Would she like me once she met me? Would we become friends? What about Dutch?* There are so many questions and, yes, worries, but this is so exciting!

Sent: Tuesday, April 12, late night
From: Nancy
To: Claire
Subject: for you
My dear Claire:

Words cannot express the absolute joy that I have experienced in our two phone conversations. Dutch and you are so much more than the light at the end of the tunnel. I so look forward to more interactions and finally to being together in person.

I'm sending you Becky Crofoot's contact information. She does not work every day, but is very good about getting back. She is a jewel and will be thrilled to hear about our connection.

As you know, I have a complete notebook of information starting back seventeen years ago (and beyond) and if there is anything in it that you or Dutch would like to see, I would be glad to scan it and send it to you. The announcement of my existence is a very big deal and I know that time and verification to take it all in is necessary.

For tonight I will say good night, and thank you for being so open and so loving.

Go well.

Love, Nancy

From: Claire
Date: April 13, early, early morning
To: Nancy

Well, I just called Becky and she was so thrilled to hear we finally connected. I thanked her so much in her involvement with you over the last few years and sticking with it until you were somehow able to find us. She said she was not going to give up until you found us! She is amazing.

I've tried to send attachments but it says they are too big. I'm going to send each one separate and we'll see how that goes.

I don't have any other pictures at home as they are all packed but this will make me start to go through some stuff. The picture that was used for the obit was actually a picture of her standing by their front door. For the obituary, the paper could only put the face in but the whole picture is what makes it. As soon as I find it, I'll send (or give you in person) a copy of that one.

I was so excited to get up this morning and already found an e-mail waiting from you. I spoke to a few of my friends last night and they are thrilled. I feel like a part of mom was brought back to me with you. I know mom is very happy that you found us and she is looking down on all of us smiling!

Thanks for not giving up until you found us! Thank your friend that went online to help you find mom that led you to us! I love you and look forward to learning more about you and sharing more about our mom! I'm so glad you had a good family and a good life and that mom found that out. Even if she had peace with it earlier as you said, I'm sure that made her feel even more assured of why she had done what she did.

I'll be talking to you soon! Give Michael a big hug and tell him to get used to it, as your sister is a hugger. My friends say that you don't know what you've gotten yourself into! That's true, but it's going to be so much fun to find out!

Take care!

Claire (your sister!)

Sent: Wednesday, April 13, late afternoon
From: Nancy
To: Claire
Subject: Us
Dear Claire:

I have been gone all day and what a wonderful surprise to find these e-mails plus from you. How adorable you all look. I love the pictures! And Dutch sent me e-mail! Just a short note, but can't help but get excited! Here we go!

Go well.

Love, Nancy

From: Claire
Date: April 13, early evening
To: Nancy

Well, I called and talked to him, but he still seems hesitant to actually contact you directly. But he wants to get together too and said anytime. I told him you're gone next week so as soon after that as it can be done! A friend of mine showed me yours and Michael's pictures on Facebook and I think you look like mom and you definitely look like you're related to us!

Sent: Wednesday, April 13, early evening
From: Nancy
To: Claire
Subject: Us
My dear Claire, my sister:

I just heard from Dutch again and I must tell you that I had to pinch myself; thinking "Did this really happen, finally after all of these years?" All day I have kept stopping and then I start smiling. I spent most of the afternoon with my friend, who was the one that found you. We spent most of the time crying. She is so pleased to have been the expediter of my dreams.

I am glad that you saw some similarities in my pictures. I was so worried that after all this, I might look more like my birth father or his family, and you would be uncomfortable with that. I adore you both already. How your mom loved you and you loved her!

And so I am coming up to see you both! As you know I will be gone next week (Mon-Fri). And next weekend is Easter. I am coming back on Friday in order to be here with Michael for Easter. I thought it might be best to come up on the weekend. That way you don't have to take much time off from your jobs. So, I am looking at Friday, May 13th through Sunday the 15th. I looked at the weekend before, but that is Mother's Day. I thought that would be fitting, but then I thought we might cry even harder all weekend and I do want to be able to talk with you and hear all that you have to say.

A month away seems a very long time, I know, but I will be out of town next week. It's time to tell you that I am writing a book. Rather I have been writing it for almost three years. It is a novel and part of the story involves a drive from LA to Boise, which I have never done. In fact, I have never been to Boise. Now why did I write a book about moving there? It came in a dream. So I called an LA friend, and said, "Interested in a road trip?" She didn't ask where, she just said, "I'm in." She is wild about driving and that will give me an opportunity to take in the drive and scenery. Does that sound crazy? Of course, it does, but I am that kind of crazy. So that cuts out a chunk of time from April 30-May 5th. I hope you don't mind waiting.

Amtrak tells me I can arrive about 4:30 pm. Should I arrive later? Are you close to the train station? And what motels/hotels are close to either one or both? I looked online, but then thought, "Better find out what would be most convenient for them." And so it begins.

Again, again, again, thank you for being so open, so gracious, so wonderful. And I thought it couldn't get any better than this!

And speaking of books, I believe that the three of us should collaborate on a book about y(our) incredible mother. What an amazing, loving life!

I will bring my notebook that is filled with 17 years of searching. Michael is anxious to meet everyone as well, but said distinctly, "Siblings first, then me!"

Go well, my dear.

From: Claire
Date: April 14, 5:30 a.m.
To: Nancy
Subject: All great news!

Another early morning. I was out all last night at swimming. Did I tell you how much I love to swim?

I have to tell you Dutch is coming around, but he's definitely a little more cautious than I am. I think he's very upset that mom did not tell us. I look at it as if she did not tell my dad she would have looked at it as a betrayal to tell us. As I stated earlier we just packed all her things away including her writings. I really feel like we might find something about you there and it has made both of us want to start going through her things. Dutch did say we need to find the journals and I agreed. I think I told you but we found a journal that my mom had kept when we found out my dad was ill. She also kept a journal when Cathy was in the car accident and the year after she died. Years ago she would keep her journals on calendars and all of those have been saved too. All her pictures are packed away too and I definitely want to get that together for you to see.

One of the cousins said you might be pulling a scam or that it was all a mistake. I have to say at first that crossed my mind and then when I really thought about it I realized you had nothing to gain and a mistake would not have this many correct facts. I told Dutch that all you want to do is hear about mom and what she was like. I told Dutch that I always wondered if I was a ½ empty glass or a ½ full kind of gal and now I know I'm a ½ full kind of gal. I want to know as much about the information you have as much as you want to know what we know and experienced with her. Just the information that she had left for you but you did not get until you were in your 40's was amazing but I could tell it was mom just by the way she wrote it. She would have wanted you to have as much information as you might have needed without knowing her. I tend to think that not a lot of women at that time probably did not give all the information she did. Maybe I'm wrong but that's definitely how (our) mom was! That cracked me up that she listed how tall her sisters were and how much they weighed! I wouldn't want my weight listed! But of course, she only listed how tall her brothers were!

The 13th of May does seem so far away, but that will give me time to compile some things together that you would like to see. As far as where to stay in Olympia, don't worry about how close you are to my house. Any place will be great. It's not going to matter how close as I'm probably just going to camp out with you! Well, I'll let you sleep if you need it but that's about it!

I'm very anxious to meet Michael too but am so glad the first meeting will just be the siblings. In my mind I'm already planning trips to the ocean! I have a friend that I told (well several actually!), but one of them wants to meet you so bad. I said I get to meet her first, as she's my sister! She laughed. Another friend said, "Maybe she's rich! How cool would that be?" I laughed and said yeah I'll tell her she should help her younger sister as mom would have wanted that and everyone laughed! Just kidding, as I don't need help. I'm doing fine so don't think I'm after you for anything either!

Okay, one more month! I can do this. I would like my feet to touch ground a little bit though so I can get ready for meeting you but I've been flying so high since we've talked that I can't come down just quite yet!

You mentioned writing a book about all of us. I love the idea of a book, but I would definitely have to be the resource and not the writer as you can see I didn't get that from mom! I write like I talk . . . I'm just all over the place! Believe me when I say that I really do talk just like I write!

Have a great day, and see you in a month!

P.S. Were you able to open our mom's story? I love it so much and wanted you to have it so much. If not let me know and I'll send it again. Talk to you later!

From: Nancy
To: Claire
Subject: What a delight you are.

This week has been such a treasure for me. All of the conversations, all of the sharing ... it is wonderful. Thank you for doing all of this.

I am sorry that I didn't mention earlier how delighted I was about y(our) mom's story. Such detail, and what an amazing family. We have no idea how difficult life was during our parents' time. Her step-mom really was precious, wasn't she? Her statement: "These are my children," sent shivers down my spine. But all the wonderful details, the stories.

I have written a cover letter to Dutch and plan to make copies of several key documents going back to the 1950 adoption degree and including y(our) mom's 1995 letter to Becky Crofoot. I am not attempting to change his mind, but I think he might find details in them that are reassuring. This all takes time to sink in and then there's an adjustment phase; just as it did for me in 1994. I kept looking at the letter for days that stated my birth mother had not died as I suspected. Would you like me to send them to you via computer or mail? Reactions vary greatly. I have known so many adopted friends. Each has a different story. Those who have searched have received so many differing responses. One family of four, who reunited, as adults were so happy, but the spouses and their children had the worst time adjusting. I get it. Change is not always welcome.

Good for the cousins in being cautious and concerned. Sad but true, there are so many scams and we all have to be careful.

I am anxious for the 13th to arrive and wish it could be sooner, but unfortunately, I had scheduled all of these trips long ago. I have an outpatient surgery scheduled the day before I come. It's minor (just a benign polyp removal) and sitting on the train will be relaxing. If I can relax for all of the excitement!

Ah, that I were the rich sister. My son would love if I were the rich mother!! And I would love that as well. But alas and alack, I am just happily retired, and making ends meet. As you know, living is expensive. Something always needs fixing. I liked working retail in the pet supply world, but I hated the fact that I never had the same schedule EVER and never knew what I was working until the week before. Plus, throwing 50 pounds of cat litter or dog food on the belt was a literal pain. Now, if I win the lottery, we will all party like rock stars!!

I too am having a hard time allowing myself to put my feet back on the ground and wait to come to Olympia. Michael keeps catching me lost in thought. He teases, "Bet I know what you're thinking about!"

Oh, do you have unlimited long distance? If not, don't hesitate to e-mail me to call you because I do!

Well, I'm going to make reservations soon for Olympia. Take care of yourself and e-mail me or call whenever you wish. If there's something more you want to know before I get there, just let me know.

Looking forward to camping out with you!

Go well.

Love, your just as crazy and loving sister, Nancy

From: Claire
Date: April 14, 7:30 p.m.
To: Nancy
Subject: Just a quick note

We both are supposed to have unlimited long distance on our cells, but feel free to call me anytime!

I definitely want to see everything that you have been collecting over the last 17 years, but no need to mail as I can just see it when you're here. I don't need to see any documents to know (as I already know you are my sister) I just want to see your path to get to us and look at everything you have. Did she give you an actual copy of the letter mom wrote? If so that will be a treasure to see and Dutch will know even more that this is real and true as you can always recognize the handwriting of family members. I think I would always know my dad's, Jack's, and Cathy's also. Especially my sister Cathy as she had such a beautiful script but very hard to read!

I told Dutch to contact Becky but he's a little funny about that too. He believes the agency could not give any information to us. I think because mom is gone, it's hard for him to have someone else say he can do this. As I said though I think he is starting to believe it, but he's hurt. So men have a harder time with this than women? I think he'll get over it. Don't worry because I think he'll be fine. It's funny when I called Becky I think she expected questions and all I could do was thank her for sticking by you all these years until you found us. She said she wouldn't have let you go until you found us! Love her too!

I'm hoping you're still going to come at 4:30 and I'll come pick you up. I've already taken that Friday afternoon off and the following Monday as I'll probably sleep all day Monday! Don't worry we'll get some sleep but it will be hard as I will be treasuring every minute with you! If you end up coming earlier, no problem as I'll be around and available anytime.

Well I'm off. Talk to you soon dear sister!

Becky's Note: *There is no way to completely prepare for a meeting with a birth relative who is also a stranger. The range of emotions is immense. Generally, one should take a deep breath and be prepared for anything. Most first meetings go very well although people are often surprised at the intensity of their emotions. Birth relatives are sometimes stunned by the adopted person's resemblance to their mother or themselves. In awkward situations, childhood pictures are welcome to help to break the ice. However, most have no trouble finding something to say.*

From: Claire
Date: April 25 at 10:50 pm
To: Nancy
Subject: So glad you called on Saturday!

And glad you're home! I so enjoyed talking to you.

I'm sure it's still going to be a great visit and I'm so pleased that Dutch wants to meet you. We all have time together and then the sisters will have time together! Now when I told you I wanted to camp out with you all weekend I really meant it but I definitely don't have a problem heading home at night and coming back in the morning or how ever is the most comfortable for you. I figure we'll just see how it goes when the 13th finally gets here!

Have a great weekend.

Sent: April 25 at 11:00 pm
From: Nancy
To: Claire
Subject: Oh, Claire, you are so cute!

Thank you so much for all of the funny e-mails, and for your kind words.

I'm so glad that I called and I enjoyed our conversation so much. I can hardly wait to be able to do this in person.

I'm glad you talked about Dutch's feelings. It's better that I know that he is having concerns and some difficulties with the announcement of "Congratulations, it's a Nancy!" As I said, I never wanted to cause any problems for either one of you. Losing a beloved parent (and the last parent particularly) is difficult enough and the grieving period is not a set amount of time. It affects everyone differently. I was 9 years old when my mom's mother died. My mother was from the second marriage and she had two older sisters, whom she adored and they adored her. All three sisters were nurses and it devastated them all that they could not save their mother. They kept her at home and took turns caring for her. When she died, they were so grief struck that they started fighting amongst themselves. One of my aunts told my mom about some small token, "You can't have that; it's not from your family!" This was the first time that my mother had ever felt that there was a division between her father and her from her sisters.

I remember this scene so well because I was right in the middle of it. My mom was sobbing with grief and hurt and dragged me out of the house. The apologies came almost immediately and the sisters resumed their loving relationship, which they had for the rest of their lives. But grief was driving both my aunts that day. It has the potential to turn us inside out as it did with my aunts and mom.

As the Beatles said, "And in the end, the love you take is equal to the love you make." I am excited about the potential of "us." I can't think of anything more fun than a camp out. It has meant so much to have had so many opportunities to share in the past few weeks (amazing isn't it? just a few weeks) and I am so looking forward to "the beginning of a beautiful friendship."

I talked to Becky Crofoot this morning and she was VERY pleased indeed. "Keep me posted," she said in closing.

Well, it's time to start my round of doctor appointments today. Hope the sun came out this afternoon in Olympia. It's trying down here.

Talk to you soon, you dear soul.

From: Claire
Date: April 25, 11:30 p.m.
To: Nancy
Subject: I'm so glad that you are so understanding!

I guess I was worried as I talked more about other things than just the "Congratulations, it's a Nancy"! I loved how you wrote that!

Well we've all had rough times and it's just how we get through them and I don't think anyone else has it way worse than anyone else unless they are homeless, dying or something else of that nature and right now he doesn't have it that bad. I think that I at times have lost patience.

I'm like you I'm so excited about the "us"! It's nice knowing too that this first time is just to really get to know each other better but that this isn't a one-time thing! We are family now! We were before too it's just that we didn't know it. I'm glad to hear that Michael is just as excited as I can tell you my husband, Dale, is really happy for me too. He always goes along with me and how I feel, and is very protective of me. I think he's really proud of how I handled this as he said it just really shows what type of person that I am. I mean I'm not angry with mom and all I want to do is meet you and start our relationship. I'm not angry with mom for not telling me as I look at that as wasted energy and besides I'm not angry. I hope that doesn't upset you (I don't think it will) but mom had her reasons. Those reasons don't exist any longer as she is not here. If she were here this would be a lot more difficult as I would still want to contact you and I would try and help her to want to meet you too. She had her reasons but we can't try to figure them out or have it affect us. I know in my heart that mom is so glad you found us and I know she's happy that you're going to hear about her. Mom has probably met your adopted family by now and they are all probably just are as excited as we are that we're going to finally meet.

I do want to hear all about your health issues though and these doctor appointments. Hope all is well there.

Love you, and talk to you soon!

From: Claire
Date: April 28, 7:42 am
To: Nancy
Subject: Just a quick note to say HI!

I'll be so busy at work the next few days; I won't have the energy to e-mail at night. But just wanted to let you know I'm still thinking of you.

Talk to you more soon! I really hope you have a great road trip next week with your friend.

Love ya!

From: Claire
Date: May 3, 8:02 pm
To: Nancy
Subject: There really is some stuff in here that is surprising!

OK, I know you're on your trip but I was just thinking about you! Hang in there, Michael, if you're reading this while she's gone, because she'll be home in a week or less!

It ends up that Dale is going to be out of town the whole weekend that you are staying here, so I'm not going to be able to camp out in your hotel room – bummer! I'll have to go feed animals at night and stay with them. During the day the little bit I have to let them out or whatever we can go together if you want. Then you can see how tiny our house is and that I wasn't exaggerating!

Hope to talk to you soon!

Love ya (Isn't that funny as I already really do)!

Claire

P.S. One of the cousins just confirmed their parents were living in Nebraska in 1949. That cousin would be glad to meet you if you're ever in his area. You will love him. Those cousins are the kids of the aunt and uncle who helped Mom when she was pregnant with you. They are all great. Dixon is the oldest son—not child but oldest. He was really excited for us! Pretty cool huh?!

Ok, now I'll talk to you later!

Sent: May 8, 9:33 pm
From: Nancy
To: Claire
Subject: You cute girl, Claire

I'm back and certainly was pleased with your e-mails awaiting me. The trip was good, we had no problems, and I came away thinking that Boise was a cool city. My friend was a great traveling companion. She was in charge of all music and sound entertainment. We had a long day driving Monday and met up with another friend in Reno at our hotel. I hadn't seen her in forever also and we had a great, albeit short, visit. The two girls had not seen one another since I left LA (16 years ago) and they had a lot to share. Tuesday we did a short drive to Winnemucca, and Wednesday brought us into Boise in the afternoon. We didn't cover the whole town, but we made a valiant attempt. I am now again inspired and plan to see this book finished this summer.

My new/old cousin's "welcome" was certainly great. Thank you for sharing that with me.

It is just days, now, sister Claire, and the excitement is building. I can hardly wait. I am sorry that I won't get to meet your guy, Dale, this time, and totally understand why you have to be at home with your critters. I look forward to meeting them too. As long as I can remember, there have been animals in my life, and I don't want to ever think about having to live without them.

Now, besides the book of my search, is there anything else you would like me to bring? Think about it.

I was going to call this weekend, but I have been away so much, I didn't want to cheat Michael out of my full attention. Because, as you know, I am leaving again soon. This day (Mother's Day) is tough for me. I was glad to be able to visit my parents' burial site last Sunday. I stayed with my friend, Carol, (who also is SOOOO excited about your response) and due to health reasons, she is not going to get back to Wisconsin this Memorial Day to decorate her parents' and sister's gravesite. So, we took two bouquets to my parents, with one representing Carol's folks. Two little old girls, crying in the beautiful California sunlight last Sunday.

Have a great, short workweek. I will talk to you this week.

From: Claire
Date: May 8, 10:38 pm
To: Nancy
Subject: So glad to hear from you and that your trip was good!

I had so planned to call you yesterday and thought the same thing that Michael sure has not had much time with you this month and that I knew I'd see you on Friday.

I had a rough weekend! My left arm went completely out on me about 3:00 in the morning Saturday. I couldn't move it and I was in extreme agony for most of Saturday. The pain finally settled down some and I could at least do some things with my arm on Sunday. Saturday morning Dale was so worried as he had to work and didn't want to leave. I didn't know what to do as I literally was in extreme pain every time I moved. Coming from someone that is almost always in pain (in my back) let me tell you that says a lot! I told Dale I needed to get to the bathroom as I was going to be sick. The pain was so bad it was making me nauseated.

It's only been this bad about five times in my life, so I knew what was coming. As he was helping me to the bathroom I knew I was going to pass out so I kind of just fell like a sack of potatoes (wasn't funny then, but that's a little amusing now). Dale was getting me a pan, wet, cold washcloths, and threatening to take me to the hospital. One of the guys that works for Dale was already there, but he had been out chasing our dog down as somehow during this she had gotten out of the house. They both of them looked down at me pathetically trying to figure out what to do. I was giving directions to Dale on how to set the bed up with a pan, washcloths and pillows stacked. He then helped me in there. His work friend wanted to also help but didn't know what to do as no one could touch my left arm without me losing it. Once he got me in there I was able to settle down.

Dale went to work making me promise I would call him if needed. I did ok during the day. I had to move out to the living room and just sit up as my back can't take it if I lay down too long! I guess you should know that physically I'm a mess! Poor Dale, he was threatening to cancel his trip but this could make him a lot of money and we could sure use it right now. I can tell you I'm tired of living in this tiny house!

The thing with my arm really sounds like what a friend went through when he first got diagnosed with rheumatoid arthritis. That's all I need! I mean with my back issues I'm learning to do things that help me feel better but if I have this that's going to mean random pain anywhere? I am going to try and get in to my doctor either Friday morning or Monday—seeing as I already have those days off. Hopefully everything will work out. The other thing that scared Dale that those symptoms also can mean heart attack and he was flipping out. He was going to cancel his trip everything. I told him no that I would be fine and that I was just glad that this didn't happen next weekend! At least if it does (God forbid) I'll hopefully be able to figure out what to do.

I really had planned on getting some pictures together for you of mom but I'm really sorry to say that hasn't happened and I can't really see it happening now before you get here. I will be getting as many pictures of her as I can though but even that is limited as most of my keepsakes are still packed. We both have a lot of stuff and there's just no room for us, the animals and our stuff, so we have a full storage unit! Our little garage is filled with our things. And in the storage unit we have most of mom's things and all of Dale's aunt's and uncle's belongings also as we also lost them in the last couple of years too. If I don't get this together by this trip I will have it soon and Dale and I can come to Portland so the guys can meet and I can show you more pictures and give you some of your own. I so wanted this ready for you this weekend and I'm so sorry that it's not going to happen. I can always mail things to you also.

I'm getting so excited for this weekend. It's going to be great! I was telling a friend of mine that I've been slowly cleaning. I am so limited with my back. Even so, I dusted one day, then cleaned up the kitchen, got the laundry all cleaned up and even vacuumed. Then this weekend happened and the place became a mess again! It's miserable having these physical difficulties. I just can't count on feeling good when I need to! If you do come over to our house at all this weekend please take that into mind.

As for you bringing anything but yourself and the papers that you have that brought you to us I'm not sure. Of course, I would love to see pictures of Michael and Forrest, and your lives together, but I also know we'll be coming to visit you too and that can also wait until then so you don't have to bring so much when you come. Just bring a few pictures of you guys and a few of you from younger days to now.

Ok what time is your train coming in? We have established that I can come and pick you up right? I'm not sure if Dutch is coming then or not but I'll find out and let you know.

This mother's day was a little hard for me too, but also it brought me more happiness than pain as I now have a new connection with mom and it is you! I can hardly wait until I see you in person and get to hold you in my arms! As I've stated probably a hundred times already, I know mom is so happy that you found us and that we can share her life with you and you can share what you know with us. It's funny because you can share things too. I knew mom loved books, stories and poems but I never would have said she collected poems and yet that was something you knew!

So you see there are things that you can share with us too that we didn't know about her more than just you. Meaning you're not the only thing about mom that we didn't know. Mom could not remember her mother really at all to tell us much but it sounds like she gave a very detailed description for you to have. I think mom must have set aside things in her mind that were so painful so that she could move forward and one of those things was also her mother. She had wanted to talk to one of her sisters once, as she didn't remember what she looked like or what her hair was like and she wanted to be told. I think you said she described all that in the letter you got. It's all still so amazing to me. I remember Dutch telling me on one of his days with mom that he found out her mother had been a principal at a school. She had never told us that before. You knew that.

At the end I think more of those things were coming back to her and her mother was probably around her too those last days. I told you it was like the room was crowded. When I asked if she could see Dad, Cathy, and John, and she was looking around like she was looking through a lot of faces and then she had a huge smile when she saw them. It was amazing!

Ok, ok, enough writing in just days I'm going to be able to tell you all this and more and I can't wait to hear all about you, your life, and your journey to us!

You know you should save these e-mails, as these might be good for your book too. Too bad our first few phone conversations weren't taped!

Love you and see you Friday! (WOW! I'm going to SEE you Friday!)

Claire

Sent: May 9, 9:30 am
From: Nancy
To: Claire
Subject: You poor dear; you've been through the ringer.

If the doctor can see you Friday, go; don't worry about what time I'm getting in (which is 4:30 pm). I can always wait. I rarely go anywhere without a book or knitting. I am so sorry that you have been having this much difficulty. Life shouldn't be this hard.

I can hardly wait to give you a huge hug (unless you are in pain). Don't worry about not having any pictures; it's us that's important. And don't worry about how your house looks. There are many, many more important things in life than cleaning house.

Dutch just sent an e-mail and asked what time the train is coming in!

Can hardly wait! Take care and hope that you are able to rest comfortably tonight.

Go well, dear sister Claire.

Love, Nancy

From: Claire
Date: May 10, 8:03 am
To: Nancy
Subject: Woe is me!

Well, when I called my doctor to make an appointment yesterday they kind of freaked out and made me go to the ER, as the symptoms were so close to heart attack. My boss at work asked me when I got my doctor's degree, as I didn't want to go. Well upon many past experiences I know the ER is a minimum of 4 hours. Which it was and my heart is fine. I have a regular appointment with my doctor on Monday so they can run some tests for the rheumatoid arthritis. I didn't know Dale was really thinking about canceling his trip because he was so worried. He can really make some money with this job and so I'm glad for him that I went. He actually got to the ER before I did, as I wanted to finish some things at work before I left. He called me here and said "Get your butt down here and forget the work!" Everyone at work was cracking up. People were offering to drive me and I said I was fine. I mean I drove to work. SHEESH!!

Needless to say brother Dutch was a little freaked out yesterday too. This was a good icebreaker for both of us though. He said that his two sons really want to meet you. I told him that's great and I figured at some point if that works for them we can go to their house and visit. I hope you don't mind but I'm going to tell him the train pick up would just for the siblings! I have always been extremely close with my nephews. I always refer to them as "my boys" and when they were little I was always "their Claire."

I guess I thought that there would never really be anyone good enough for either one of them, but I was so wrong. They have wonderful wives and I consider them "mine" as well. Both have the cutest kids (don't we all say that about "our" kids?). They both remember Mom and were really close with her. We were all so worried about how to tell them when she was gone. I don't think they ever really did too much but I'm sure they were told she is in Heaven. One is four and the other six. I am so excited for you to meet them all!

Ok, well, the arm feels pretty darn good today and I have an appointment with my regular doctor on Monday so everything is good! It's going to be hard with Dale gone, as I'll really miss him but this job pays really well so it will all be worth it.

I won't be missing a minute of time with you (well except when I have to go home and take care of the pets) so here we go: three more days! I'm so excited. Thank Michael for letting you take one more weekend away with your sibs! You sure have been away from him a lot the last month and I tend to think that's probably not the norm. Well that's just my guess anyway.

See you soon! Very soon! So soon that my heart is already ready to burst! That's probably why they thought it was a heart attack as my heart is definitely going haywire with all the excitement!

Love ya!

Claire

Sent: May 10, 3:30 pm
From: Nancy
To: Claire
Subject: You poor thing

Claire:

I know you didn't want to, but I am so glad that you sought medical attention yesterday. Normal results are always the preferred diagnosis. But I know what you mean, you had a bad Sunday, but then you started to feel better on Monday, and everyone else around you is freaking out and you want to say, "What?!!!" But it's always harder for those around us, because they feel so helpless.

Six years ago when the spots were found on my pancreas, everyone started talking to me in hushed tones, telling me what a good patient I was. I knew what was up, and started saying, "I don't have cancer, folks. I don't have time for cancer." But it took a lot more to convince Michael that I was not checking out on him. Tell Dale that although I will miss meeting him, I won't let you suffer. I am a big advocate for seeking medical attention. Wherever our visit takes place, we are going to have time this weekend. I can talk to you, sitting alongside a gurney, just as well as in a hotel room or your house.

Perfectly fine with me for siblings at the train. Anything you want to do is fine. I will happily look forward to meeting everyone.

ONLY THREE MORE DAYS!! Ta Dah!!

Tomorrow I'm on clear fluids only (yuck) and then Thursday the vaginal polyp comes off! It looks and acts totally benign; basically it's just an annoyance that will soon not be my problem! And then I'm on my way to our future!

Continue to have a good day, sister Claire.

Love, Nancy

From: Claire
Date: May 10, 8:38 pm
To: Nancy
Subject: Thanks!

One last quick note. Dutch is coming to the train too so it will be all the siblings! He agreed that he didn't want you to be overwhelmed! That wasn't my worry. I just wanted the siblings to meet first! As far as I'm concerned the whole thing is a little overwhelming but it is a good overwhelming. We'll go to dinner with them or something sometime this weekend. We'll decide that when you get here.

Ok I'll pray for you tomorrow and Thursday and I will also pray that you won't be uncomfortable on your trip over.

Love you and see you Friday! Wow Friday! I'm so happy!!!

Sent: May 11, 3:34 pm
From: Nancy
To: Claire
Subject: My wonderful husband

Hello, Claire: Since you don't get to meet him yet, I thought that you would enjoy going to the website Reverbnation.com and searching for Bridge City Blues Band. This way you can hear Michael Feldman and the band. They have about 6 songs on it. Michael sings and plays harmonica. Michael's hair is the most white of anyone's.

If blues isn't your thing, it won't be that much fun, but still it's fun to know this about Michael Feldman.

Love, Nancy

From: Claire
Date: May 11, 4:00 pm
To: Nancy
Subject: Michael's band

I pulled it up but can't play the songs. I'll send this to Dutch as maybe he can figure it out. Do you have to have Internet access to hear the songs? I could see the pictures and everything and kept clicking on songs but they wouldn't play! DARN!! That is way cool! I'm an ok blues fan but Dale and Dutch just love it! They will be very excited!!

Sent: May 11, 4:15 pm
From: Nancy
To: Claire
Subject: Michael's band

I also sent an e-mail to you from the site. Hope it works too. I must admit that the man is really good and it IS so cool that he's good at this and loves doing it. And no one ever knew that he had such a good voice!

I, on the other hand, have a HORRIBLE voice. Twice a month, Michael does a jam, and I knit!

Love, Nancy

From: Claire
Date: May 11, 6:30 pm
To: Nancy
Subject: Musical star

Well, I used to be a soprano. Dutch and I sang in the church choir when we were young. Love singing but I have a horrible voice now! I blame the smoking but I always remember the Brown family singing "Happy Birthday" and that was a sorry song to hear us sing—boo hoo.

I learned knitting in junior high but never really took it up and can't really do any of it now.

That is so exciting about Michael! Dale and I will definitely be planning at least one of our trips around him playing so we can hear it! Dale's pretty excited too that we can take a trip up to Portland! I have friends on the alert trying to find out how I can hear his songs! This is way exciting! Thanks for sharing that!

Most of my friends are sorry you didn't get to meet mom too but I tell them that we are just so excited at what we have now that we can't feel bad about what would have, could have, should have happened!

You know if you keep answering me back I'm going to keep responding to you! I can't help it as all I want to do is talk to you, see you, and hug you big time!!

See you! Love you! Glad you found me! Glad you found us!

Claire

From: Claire
Date: May 11, 7:30 pm
To: Nancy
Subject: The band

I finally heard them! They are great! This is so exciting! Meeting my sister who is writing a book and married to a famous blues artist! I'm in heaven!

TWO MORE DAYS!!!!!!

Well, the news about Michael being a bluesman and his being able to hear his music has been the thing that finally seems to have gotten Dutch so excited! He then asked what else I knew about you and I went back through our e-mails and started sharing a lot with him. I also told him that you get very excited and happy every time that he sends you an e-mail.

This is going to be good, Nancy, as it won't just be you and me (which I would have still loved) but Dutch I think will really be involved! Dutch had thought about the Spaghetti Factory as a fun place to go to dinner with the kids (which we'll probably still do if you're ok with spaghetti) but I did tell him there is one in Portland and that they all looked alike. It's funny though because Dutch lived in Portland about 28–30 years ago for about a year or so and he didn't know that. Did you live in Portland then?

Well enjoy your liquids today! I'll be thinking of you and shooting little prayers up for you today and tomorrow (well just for everyday)!

I love you and see you in 2 days!

Claire

P.S. Dale just left last night and I already miss him!

Sent: May 11, 9 pm
From: Nancy
To: Claire
Subject: TWO MORE DAYS INDEED!!!!!!!!!!

So, so pleased that Dutch enjoyed Michael's music and that it got him excited.

I agree that this is all going to be good! I LOVE the Spaghetti Factory. The funny thing is that I have not been to the one in Portland. We used to meet friends at the Hollywood (L.A. Hollywood, not Portland) one as it was half way in between our two houses. But I think Spaghetti Factory sounds great!

Michael and I moved to Portland 16 years ago, so we missed Dutch by a few years. We met in L.A. at a job in 1974, but did not get involved until 1976. We married in 1977, and were in the South Bay part of LA, moving many times, until 1995, when we moved to Portland. I'm going to do a little history for both of you on me, Michael and Forrest.

Again, I'm sorry that I am going to miss meeting Dale, but I know you said it was going to be a big help that he took this job. I know it's hard. Being apart sucks, but homecomings are the best!

Love you back and see you in two days!

Love, Nancy

From: Claire
Date: May 12, 7:00 am
To: Nancy
Subject: ONE MORE DAY!!

I know that you've got your procedure today; my prayers and love are with you! And then, it's tomorrow and you'll be here! Just be ready as you're going to be given a big hug, and then we'll chat and we'll laugh. There is probably going to be some tears too but it is going to be the BEST and only the beginning of our beautiful relationship. I'm sorry mom won't be here to enjoy this but believe me, Nancy, she's going to be watching over us all and she's very happy!

One more day! We can get through this! I'll see you soon!

Love ya,
Claire

The procedure went fine with only minimal discomfort, but it's true, the "forget it drugs" were a big help. The next morning I was literally in a daze on the car ride to the train station. Michael kept saying things like, "Now if for any reason you're uncomfortable or it doesn't go well, you call me, and I will get you home as soon as possible. Promise me, you won't hesitate to call me. If I need to, I will just drive there and bring you home. I won't leave you stranded. Promise me, you will call."

I promised. I was nervous, but I wasn't afraid that things wouldn't work out. I had decided that everything was going to be fine. Maybe it wouldn't be super fine, but it would be fine. I had train tickets both ways, and my own hotel room. I knew that there were no guarantees, but I wasn't worried. But I was almost dumb struck. Was it dopiness from the day before? Whatever it was I calmly knitted when I couldn't concentrate to read all the way to Olympia/Lacey.

My heart was really pounding when I stepped off the train. The crowd of people waiting seemed huge, but I attributed it to my nerves. *What if they decided not to come?* I worried. Then I heard a woman's voice call my name. I looked to my right and saw a man and a woman staring at me. The woman looked familiar and she had tears in her eyes. *Did she look familiar because she looked like me?* The man wiped his eyes as well. I remembered something Becky had said about every meeting had a strong emotional component to it. We paused for a second and then they scooped me into their arms while exclaiming, "Oh, my god, you've got Mom's eyes! You are so our sister!"

It was a weekend filled with just about every emotion possible. I should correct that. There were no feelings of hatred, envy, or revenge. Claire and I spent the most time together that weekend. She wanted to share so much with me. I stayed in a hotel and the first night she stayed late, and as we were talking across from one another, I noticed something about her that was startling.

We look alike. I could actually see myself in her. We spent a lot of time passing the Kleenex box back and forth while we talked.

My story continues, and yet, in many ways it is just beginning where this book concludes. My sister, Claire, had prepared an envelope of information for me to read at my hotel during that first visit. There were many facts about my birth mother's family and photographs. I could see myself in many of the faces. An astounding discovery was that I was born on my birth mother's mother's birthday. What a startling coincidence that must have been for my birth mother.

For the first time in my life, I am a sister. Seriously, even after two years, this still blows my mind. But I don't delude myself into thinking that I can just move right into my birth mother's family. They are established in their lifestyles and holiday traditions. From the beginning, I wanted my siblings and their families to know that "we" began in April 2011, and I did not expect anything from them. All I asked for originally was some time and information from them. If we didn't click, I would understand. If we did click, then we could make it up as we went along. And that's what we've done.

Holidays are for families, but we've had plenty of times together for festivals, concerts, and just plain visiting weekends. My sister and her husband, Dale, have known one another since junior high school. Over the years, he has spent a lot of time with her family. He says that every time I laugh, he hears my birth mother's laugh. He said that at first it was startling, but now he takes great comfort in it.

I'm very lucky in that my siblings do not live far from me. We were able to meet soon after we discovered one another's existence and that, too, has added a special dimension to our relationship. We learn something more every time we are together. And we're just beginning.

The End of the Beginning

"Now this is not the end. It is not even the beginning of the end. But, it is, perhaps, the end of the beginning."
Winston Churchill

Becky's Epilogue

One of the rewarding parts of post adoption work is the opportunity to have long relationships with people even though it may be a long distance relationship. Nancy entered my world in 1994 and simply stayed there. I had worked many years as a caseworker for the Nebraska Children's Home Society when she appeared. She dropped in and out but always reappeared. Like many adopted people, she carefully continued stepping into an unknown aspect of her life. I always knew that she would be back.

Nancy's letters were welcome because they were interesting and challenging to me as a caseworker. Likewise, I truly enjoyed talking to her on the phone. I often found myself waiting for several days to respond to her contacts in order to find the time to properly address her questions and thoughts. It was, and continues to be, an adventure for both of us.

Nancy approached me with the idea of making her story into a book just as I was about to retire from casework. I was intrigued, as her story is a good illustration of the various stages that adopted people experience when they probe into their history. Her story is also her birth mother's story. It shows the anger and fear that many of the birth mothers from the past feel when the door to the past is reopened. Sadly, there are still many birth mothers out there who feel the same way. Finally, Nancy's story is a tribute to her adoptive parents who not only provided her with love and security but also an uncomplicated sense of adoption.

The reactions of Nancy's siblings are also typical of many birth families. Some people are delighted to discover a birth sibling (like Claire) and others have mixed feelings (as Dutch did). Many are sad that their mother was not able to share that part of her early life but some are angry. It is not an easy experience for a family.

Things have changed enormously since 1949, and open adoption is now the norm. Although it is not without problems, the end result is a much healthier climate for an adopted person than the secrecy of the past.

There are people who should be mentioned for their assistance in the writing of this book. Several of the staff at the Nebraska Children's Home Society deserve many thanks for their usual support: Kim Anderson, my former supervisor, for her advice and never-ending patience and understanding; Kathy Hoyt and Kim Schenkelberg for their assistance in digging up details; and Karen Authier, Executive Director, for her support and belief that this story is relevant to the work of the Nebraska Children's Home Society.

Finally, to all of the adopted persons and members of birth families, especially birth mothers, I certainly owe a great deal of gratitude for the lessons they have taught me through the years, and to Nancy, thus your story continues. As you often say, "Go well, my friend."

Rebecca Crofoot

Nancy's Epilogue

I have never won an Academy Award and, in fact, have never been nominated. But everyone who knows me well knows that I write an acceptance speech every year, just in case I get written in! So hold back the warning music, I want to thank many people.

This book could not have been written as well without my coauthor, Rebecca Crofoot. Being able to use our actual letters makes it unique. My discovery, search, adventure, journey, and growth were beautifully facilitated thanks to Becky and the Nebraska Children's Home Society, whom I consider my alma mater. Becky never lost her professionalism, but she was always warm and supportive of me, whether in letters, on the phone, or in person. I made a life-long friend in Becky, and I treasure our friendship. And the Nebraska Children's Home Society gave me the charmed life that I have had since my parents got me.

My husband, Michael, completely supported me from the beginning on my search. "Whatever you want to do, Nancy." He has always been there, either listening to me (or pretending to do so) or giving me his "take" on what was happening. Every step of the way, Michael has been my rock. All love to you, Michael.

My friends, Carol Taipale and Linda Florentine, listened, listened, and listened. They made helpful comments, cried with me, and celebrated with me. They are simply the best, and I am the grand poobah at picking the best of friends. Hug, hug, kiss, kiss.

My longtime friend, Barbara Rowan, who created all of the greeting cards used in this book. Thank you for allowing your beautiful work to be included in this book.

My son, Forrest Cole, because I love you and this is your legacy as well. Go well and be safe.

To my siblings: Thank you for taking a chance and welcoming me into your lives.

To my family—grandparents, aunts, uncles, cousins, cousins, and cousins—no one made me feel anything but accepted and loved.

To my parents:

For my birth mother, it's a simple statement. Thank you for giving me life. "Our" beginning was a terrible time for you. But you did a wonderful thing for me.

For my mom and dad, Lucille and George Kacirek. You gave me the most incredible life. I grew up believing that being adopted and loved were the same thing. You showed me every day that I was adored. You truly made me believe that I was a special individual, who could do whatever I set out to do. And you were such adoring and involved grandparents. I never wondered who my real parents were—they were right in front of me. I miss you so much.

My family: Grandpa and Grandma Kacirek; my mom Lucille Kacirek, my horse King, Uncle John, me, and my dad George Kacirek.

12924013R00109

Made in the USA
San Bernardino, CA
04 July 2014